Company's Coming

Air Frying
Made Simple

Billey • Markakis • Pirk • Darcy

Distributed by
Canada Book Distributors
www.canadabookdistributors.com
www.companyscoming.com
Tel: 1-800-661-9017

Library and Archives Canada Cataloguing in Publication

Title: Air frying made simple / Billey, Markakis, Pirk, Darcy.
Other titles: Company's Coming
Names: Billey, Ashley, author. | Markakis, Toni, author. | Pirk, Wendy, 1973– author. | Darcy, James, 1956– author.
Description: Includes index.
Identifiers: Canadiana 20210159278 | ISBN 9781772070699 (softcover)
Subjects: LCSH: Hot air frying. | LCSH: Quick and easy cooking. | LCGFT: Cookbooks.
Classification: LCC TX689 .B55 2021 | DDC 641.7/7—dc23

All cover photos by Company's Coming except: from GettyImages: zstockphotos
(*front flap*)

All inside photos by Company's Coming except: from GettyImages: ahirao_photo, 117; ALLEKO, 61; alpaksoy, 99; badmanproduction, 13; bhofack2, 37, 83, 135, 159; Cogent-Marketing, 53; Divaneth-Dias, 185; Edalin, 87; EricFerguson, 179; EzumeImages, 11; gorchittza2012, 79; HannamariaH, 113; IgorDutina, 19; iuliia_n, 63; jackmalipan, 77; JoeGough, 97; Lizzy Komen, 161; Kondor83, 109; Panagiotis Kyriakos, 25; Lisovskaya, 55; loooby, 81; Manuta, 189; OlgaMiltsova, 123; rez-art, 67; robynmac, 149; rozmarina, 17; sailfasterman, 151; siims, 139; tarras79, 6; Tomophafan, 15; TonySoto, 73; TorriPhoto, 173; Charles Wollertz, 175; zkruger, 89; zstockphotos, 107.

We acknowledge the financial support of the Government of Canada.
Nous reconnaissons l'appui financier du gouvernement du Canada.

Funded by the Government of Canada
Financé par le gouvernement du Canada | **Canadä**

PC: 38-1

Table of Contents

The Jean Paré Story

Jean Paré (pronounced "jeen PAIR-ee") grew up understanding that the combination of family, friends and home cooking is the best recipe for a good life. When Jean left home, she took with her a love of cooking, many family recipes and an intriguing desire to read cookbooks as if they were novels!

"Never share a recipe you wouldn't use yourself."

When her four children had all reached school age, Jean volunteered to cater the 50th anniversary celebration of the Vermilion School of Agriculture, now Lakeland College, in Alberta, Canada. Working from her home, Jean prepared a dinner for more than 1,000 people and from there launched a flourishing catering operation that continued for more than 18 years.

As requests for her recipes increased, Jean was often asked, "Why don't you write a cookbook?" The release of *150 Delicious Squares* on April 14, 1981, marked the debut of what would soon turn into one of the world's most popular cookbook series.

Company's Coming cookbooks are distributed in Canada, the United States, Australia and other world markets. Bestsellers many times over in English, Company's Coming cookbooks have also been published in French and Spanish.

Familiar and trusted in home kitchens around the world, Company's Coming cookbooks are offered in a variety of formats. Highly regarded as kitchen workbooks, the softcover Original Series, with its lay-flat plastic comb binding, is still a favourite among home cooks.

Jean Paré's approach to cooking has always called for quick and easy recipes using everyday ingredients. That view served her well, and the tradition continues in the Practical Gourmet series.

Jean's Golden Rule of Cooking is: Never share a recipe you wouldn't use yourself. It's an approach that has worked—millions of times over!

Introduction

The air fryer comes to Company's Coming cookbooks! We are excited to bring you this collection of recipes for one of the most versatile appliances we've had the pleasure of working with. We had a lot of fun developing creative new recipes for this handy appliance, and we know you will love the results.

We do have to admit, however, that it was a bit tricky to produce an air fryer cookbook that can be used by anyone, because not all air fryers are created equal. Air fryer appliances have been around for years, but they are currently enjoying a surge in popularity, and many companies have jumped on the air-fryer manufacturing bandwagon. The result is a wide variety of machines with different capabilities and functionality. Some machines are dedicated air fryers, whose sole purpose is cooking air-fried food, whereas other machines are combo units that are also toaster ovens, dehydrators or even rotisserie ovens!

Even among dedicated air fryers there is a great deal of variety. Some have circular baskets and some are square, which determines the types of foods that will fit in your machine. Some have short but deep baskets that can hold a whole chicken, whereas others have longer shallow baskets that might fit a half chicken—with a little creative fiddling. In some models, the air-fryer drawer is removable while in others it is not. Some load from the top while others load from the front. You get the picture. And so, understanding your specific air fryer's quirks and limitations will help you get the most out of your machine.

In developing the recipes for this book, we tested both dedicated and combo air fryers, and the clear favourite was the dedicated air fryer. It outperformed the combo units in both performance and consistency. However, the combo units we used did not have a controllable temperature setting; they had a single air-fryer setting of 400°F (200°C). In writing this book, we geared the instructions to the dedicated air fryer, but we added instructions for each recipe for those cooks using a combo unit. More recently, we have been experimenting with combo units that have adjustable temperature settings, and we have found them to be comparable to many of the dedicated air fryers we tried. That's great news for those of us who do not have the counter space for yet another kitchen appliance! And this is an appliance that definitely deserves space in your kitchen!

Why Air Fry?

The original purpose of the air fryer was to cook traditionally deep-fried foods in a healthier way with less fat, and all air fryers deliver on that front! That reason alone would be enough to win over deep-fried food afficionados, but the air fryer has so much more to offer!

Air-fried food doesn't get soggy from absorbing too much oil, which can happen with deep-frying when the oil is not hot enough.

Another great selling feature? Less mess! Cleanup is much easier with an air fryer. There are no messy oil splatters or the need to dispose of a vat of used cooking oil. Simply wipe down the insides of the machine, and you're done!

It is also safer than deep frying because you don't have to deal with the aforementioned vat of hot oil. No need to keep a close eye on the hot oil as your food is cooking. In fact, cooking with an air fryer is super convenient because, other than occasionally flipping or moving the food around a little, you can pretty much walk away and leave the machine alone to do the cooking for you.

These machines are extremely versatile. Sure, they excel at traditionally deep-fried foods, but they also do an amazing job with pretty much any food you would bake or roast in your oven. We cooked everything from a duck breast or turkey breast to cookies and lava cakes with great success!

You won't mind firing up the air fryer even on the hottest summer day because it won't heat up your kitchen the way a conventional oven does. It also uses much less energy than your oven, saving you money on your electricity bills.

The air fryer also comes in handy when your oven is already occupied, and you want to whip up a tasty side or dessert to go along with your meal.

This appliance is also great for reheating leftovers. With an air fryer, the days of soggy reheated pizza are over. Pizza reheated in the air fryer is every bit as delicious and crispy as it was when it was freshly cooked. The same can be said for most meant-to-be crispy leftovers, including fries, onion rings, chicken nuggets and the like.

Also because these machines are relatively small and portable, they are perfect for smaller spaces such as dorm rooms or small apartments with tiny kitchens. You can even take one along on a road trip to cook your favourite foods in a hotel room or in your RV.

How an Air Fryer Works

An air fryer is basically a super convection oven. It doesn't really "fry" the food at all. A convection fan blows superheated air around the food, which evaporates any moisture released from the food as it cooks. The end result is crispy, golden brown food that rivals its deep-fried counterparts in both taste and texture.

Although these machines were developed as healthy alternatives to deep-frying food, they do an amazing job cooking all types of foods, from frittatas to cheesecakes.

The Importance of Oil

One of the most common misconceptions we have heard about the air fryer is that is replaces the need for oil. Not true. Sure, you need a lot less oil in an air fryer than you would for its deep-fried counterpart, but that doesn't mean NO oil. In our recipe testing, we discovered that a light spray of oil really improved the quality of the end result. Food that was lightly sprayed with cooking oil came out crispier and browned better.

Be mindful of the type of oil you choose, though. You'll want to use an oil with a high smoke point, such as canola, sunflower or peanut oil. Avocado oil works especially well in an air fryer, but it is pricey.

We recommend filling a spritzer bottle with your choice of oil instead of using store-bought aerosol cooking sprays. It's more cost effective and will allow you to avoid questionable ingredients that can be found in many commercially prepared cooking sprays. It's also cleaner. Many of the aerosol sprays have a wide spraying radius or poor directional control, so you end up spraying a lot more than just the food. Most manufacturers advise against using aerosol cooking sprays in their machines because chemicals in the spray can degrade the air fryer's non-stick coating.

Which brings us to our next point. NEVER spray oil onto food while it is in the air fryer. Always remove the tray or basket first. Not only will the oil gunk up the inside of your air fryer, but it will also cause your machine to smoke excessively and can lead to potentially dangerous flare-ups, especially if you are using aerosol cooking sprays.

Tips for Success

There is a definite learning curve when you first start using an air fryer. While we would rather not admit to how many fails we had in our early days of testing, we are happy to pass on the knowledge we acquired to help prevent you from making the same mistakes we did:

- Food cooks more quickly and at lower temperatures than you are used to in a conventional oven, so keep a close eye on your food until you get used to your machine. There is a not-so-fine line between yummy brown and TOO brown (i.e. burnt). Things brown quickly in an air fryer, so be vigilant.

- Don't add too much food to the basket. The air fryer uses hot air to cook the food, so the air must be able to circulate freely. If you add too much food to the basket, the pieces tend to crowd each other, and the air cannot flow around them. The end result will be a batch of soggy food instead of the crispy results you were hoping for. You are better off cooking your food in batches than overloading your basket.

- If you are cooking loose items, such as fries or chips, make sure they are in a single layer so that everything cooks evenly.

- Shake loose items (again, like fries or chips) so they cook evenly, otherwise the ones in the middle might not crisp up, and the outer ones might overcook.

- Flip other foods, like chicken fingers, halfway through to ensure the tops and bottoms are cooked evenly. You can get away with not flipping, if you must, but we found that food came out crispier when it was flipped.

- Most recipes instruct you to move your food around to ensure even cooking, but there are a few instances when you'll want to leave the food alone and let the air fryer do its job undisturbed. This instruction is usually given when the coating is delicate and can crumble if disturbed, or if the structural integrity of the dish might be compromised by opening the door or moving the basket or tray (think of a souffle collapsing when the oven door is opened). Follow the recipe instructions carefully.

- Keep your air fryer clean. We recommend cleaning it out well after every use. Over time, air-fried food can leave a buildup of oil on the inside, causing your machine to smoke excessively as it cooks. The same can be said for the racks and baskets. Wash them well after each use to ensure oil does not build up and cause a smoking hazard.

- We do not recommend lining your air fryer basket with foil. In fact, some of the models that we used specifically warned against doing so because it could affect the temperature regulation of the machine and could even be a fire hazard. If you want to minimize cleanup, use parchment paper that is made specifically for the air fryer. It is available online.

Crispy Beef Ravioli

These deliciously crispy ravioli are perfect for dipping in to a ramekin of warm marinara sauce. Sprinkle with Parmesan cheese and fresh herbs for an attractive presentation.

All-purpose flour	1/3 cup	75 mL
Salt	1 tsp.	5 mL
Black pepper	1/2 tsp.	2 mL
Onion powder	1/2 tsp.	2 mL
Large egg	1	1
Milk	1/4 cup	60 mL
Seasoned Italian bread crumbs	1 1/2 cups	375 mL
Fresh beef ravioli	28	28

Combine first 4 ingredients in a shallow bowl.

Beat egg and milk together in a bowl.

Place bread crumbs in another shallow bowl.

Coat ravioli in flour mixture, shaking off any excess. Dip into egg mixture and place in breadcrumbs, turning until evenly coated. Spray with vegetable oil spray. Transfer to air fryer basket, placing them as close together as possible. Cook at 400°F (200°C) until ravioli are crispy and brown, about 6 minutes, flipping halfway through. Let cool for 5 minutes before serving. Makes 28 ravioli.

Combo air fryer: Cook for 8 minutes, flipping halfway through.

4 raviolis: 260 Calories ; 6 g Total Fat (0.5 g Mono, 0.5 g Poly, 2.5 g Sat); 65 mg Cholesterol; 40 g Carbohydrate (2 g Fibre, 3 g Sugar); 11 g Protein; 730 mg Sodium

Papas Rellenas

Breaded potato bundles stuffed with a savoury meat sauce. This recipe works best when your mashed potatoes are chilled, so plan accordingly. You made need to cook in batches.

Medium yellow potatoes, peeled, diced	5	5
Unsalted butter	1/4 cup	60 mL
Garlic powder	1 tsp.	5 mL
Whole milk	1/4 cup	60 mL
Salt	1/2 tsp.	2 mL
Black pepper	1/4 tsp.	1 mL
Egg yolks, fork-beaten, whites reserved	2	2
Olive oil	3 tbsp.	45 mL
Medium white onion, diced	1	1
Medium green pepper, diced	1	1
Lean ground beef	2 cups	500 mL
Garlic cloves, minced	4	4
Paprika	1/2 tsp.	2 mL
Tomato sauce	1/4 cup	60 mL
Ground cumin	1 tsp.	5 mL
Ground cinnamon	1/4 tsp.	1 mL
Ground cloves	1/8 tsp.	0.5 mL
Dried oregano	1 tsp.	5 mL
Salt	1/2 tsp.	2 mL
Black pepper	1/2 tsp.	2 mL
Capers	3 tbsp.	45 mL
Raisins	3 cups	750 mL
All-purpose flour	1/4 cup	60 mL
Dry bread crumbs (see Tip, page 134)	1 cup	250 mL
Large egg, beaten	1	1
Reserved egg whites, fork-beaten	2	2

Bring potatoes to a boil in a large saucepan of salted water. Reduce heat and cook, covered, for 20 minutes or until tender. Drain.

Add butter, garlic powder and milk and mash well. Stir in salt, pepper and egg yolks. Cool in refrigerator until stiff.

Heat oil in a large frying pan on medium-high. Add onion and green pepper and cook for 5 minutes. Stir in ground beef, garlic and paprika. Using a potato masher, mash mixture until well combined.

Stir in next 7 ingredients. Reduce heat to a simmer and cook for 15 minutes. Add raisins and capers and simmer for 5 minutes.

Combine flour and bread crumbs in a small bowl. Combine egg whites and remaining egg in a shallow bowl. Form cold potato mixture into balls, using about 1/4 cup (60 mL) for each. Flatten balls slightly, place 2 tbsp. (30 mL) beef mixture in centre and reform ball to enclose filling. Roll each ball in egg mixture and then coat in bread crumbs. Cook at 325°F (160°C) for 16 minutes or until browned around edges. You may need to flip them halfway through so they brown evenly. Makes 24 balls.

Combo air fryer: Cook for 16 to 18 minutes, flipping halfway through.

2 papas rellenas: 430 Calories; 14 g Total Fat (6 g Mono, 1 g Poly, 6 g Sat); 85 mg Cholesterol; 59 g Carbohydrate (5 g Fibre, 31 g Sugar); 14 g Protein; 450 mg Sodium

Spring Rolls

These tasty spring rolls are great on their own or paired with your favourite dipping sauce. We like peanut sauce or a sweet chili sauce, but sweet and sour is great too. The rolls are easier to make when the filling is cool, so place it in the fridge for about an hour to speed up the cooling process if you prefer.

Dried shiitake mushroom pieces	15	15
Mirin	1 tbsp.	15 mL
Pure sesame oil	1 tsp.	5 mL
Cornstarch	1/2 tsp.	2 mL
Salt	1/2 tsp.	2 mL
Ground pork	3/4 lb.	340 g
Olive oil	2 tbsp.	30 mL
Garlic cloves, diced	2	2
Carrot, peeled and sliced into thin strips	1	1
Diced canned bamboo shoots	3 tbsp.	45 mL
Kale, shredded	3/4 cup	175 mL
Mirin	1 tbsp.	15 mL
Soy sauce	2 tbsp.	30 mL
Sesame oil	1 tbsp.	15 mL
Salt	1/2 tsp.	2 mL
Granulated sugar	1/4 tsp.	1 mL
Cornstarch	2 tbsp.	30 mL
Cold water	3 tbsp.	45 mL
Cornstarch	1/2 tbsp.	7 mL
Cold water	1 tbsp.	15 mL
Spring roll wrappers (8 inch, 20 cm, squares)	20	20

Soak mushrooms in 3/4 cup (175 mL) hot water for 15 minutes.

Combine next 4 ingredients in a large bowl. Add pork and stir to coat. Let stand, covered, in refrigerator for 30 minutes.

Heat oil in a large frying pan on high. Remove pork from marinade, discarding any remaining marinade. Add pork to pan and cook until browned, about 7 minutes. Add garlic, mushrooms and carrot and cook for 1 minute. Add next 3 ingredients and cook for 2 minutes.

Add next 4 ingredients and 3 tbsp. (45 mL) reserved mushroom water and simmer for 7 minutes or until water is evaporated.

Combine cornstarch and cold water in a small cup until dissolved. Add to pan and cook until liquid is evaporated. Transfer mixture to a large, shallow bowl and let cool.

Combine remaining cornstarch and water, stirring until dissolved.

Place a spring roll wrapper on a clean surface, with a corner facing toward you. Place 2 tbsp. (30 mL) filling on wrapper and roll once to enclose filling. Fold in both sides and continue rolling, ensuring your spring roll is tight. Brush cornstarch mixture on corner of last fold and press to seal. Repeat with remaining wrappers and filling. Cook at 325°F (160°C) for 12 minutes. Makes 20 spring rolls.

Combo air fryer: Cook for 12 minutes, flipping halfway through.

1 spring roll: 120 Calories; 6 g Total Fat (3 g Mono, 1 g Poly, 1.5 g Sat); 10 mg Cholesterol; 11 g Carbohydrate (2 g Fibre, 2 g Sugar); 4 g Protein; 320 mg Sodium

Pork Potstickers

The air fryer makes these delicious dumplings perfectly crispy. Although the dipping sauce is not strictly necessary, we highly recommend serving it alongside your potstickers for an amazing taste experience.

Sesame oil	1 tbsp.	15 mL
Finely chopped napa cabbage	1 cup	250 mL
Finely chopped shiitaki or cremini mushrooms	1/2 cup	125 mL
Water chestnuts, finely chopped	1/4 cup	60 mL
Chopped fresh chives	1 tbsp.	15 mL
Garlic cloves, minced	2	2
Finely grated ginger root	1 tsp.	5 mL
Large egg white, fork beaten	1	1
Ground pork	3/4 lb.	340 g
Soy sauce	2 tsp.	10 mL
Corn starch	1 tsp.	5 mL
Round dumpling wrappers, thawed if necessary	30	30
Soy sauce	1/4 cup	60 mL
Rice vinegar	2 tbsp.	30 mL
Mirin	2 tbsp.	30 mL
Water	2 tbsp.	30 mL
Garlic cloves, minced	2	2
Olive oil	2 tsp.	10 mL
Ginger, minced	1 tsp.	5 mL
Dried crushed chilies	1/4 tsp.	1 mL
Sesame seeds	2 tsp.	10 mL

Heat sesame oil in a medium frying pan on medium. Add next 6 ingredients and cook for 3 minutes until cabbage is wilted and moisture is evaporated. Cool slightly.

Stir in next 4 ingredients. Spoon about 1 1/2 tbsp. (22 mL) of filling into centre of half of wrapper. Moisten edges with water. Fold wrapper in half to make a half moon shape and close, pressing edges to seal. Wet outside edge of both sides of seams and crimp into little folds to seal. Set aside and repeat with remaining wrappers. Spray evenly with vegetable oil spray. Transfer half of potstickers to air fryer basket in one layer. Cook at 350°F (175°C) for 7 minutes, flipping halfway through. Transfer to a plate lined with foil to keep warm. Repeat with remaining potstickers.

For the dipping sauce, whisk remaining 8 ingredients in a small bowl. Set aside for 30 minutes to allow flavours to blend. Garnish with sesame seeds. Serve with potstickers. Makes 30 potstickers.

Combo air fryer: Cook for 9 minutes, flipping halfway through.

3 potstickers with 1 tbsp. (15 mL) dipping sauce: 140 Calories; 10 g Total Fat (4.5 g Mono, 1.5 g Poly, 3 g Sat); 25 mg Cholesterol; 4 g Carbohydrate (0 g Fibre, 2 g Sugar); 7 g Protein; 460 mg Sodium

Honey Garlic Chicken Wings

Crispy, sticky and just a touch sweet, just like a chicken wing should be! Break out the napkins, because things are going to get messy!

Water	1/2 cup	125 mL
Fresh lemon juice	1/2 cup	125 mL
Liquid honey	1/4 cup	60 mL
Ketchup	3 tbsp.	45 mL
Garlic cloves, minced	3	3
Grated ginger root	1 tsp.	5 mL
Salt	1 tsp.	5 mL
Chicken wings, both drumettes and winglets	3 lbs.	1.4 kg
Butter, melted	1/4 cup	60 mL

Heat first 7 ingredients in a small pot just to a boil. Stir and remove from heat.

Place chicken wings in a large resealable plastic bag. Pour marinade over top. Seal bag and marinate, in refrigerator, for at least 1 hour or up to 4 hours, turning frequently.

Remove chicken wings from marinade and transfer to a large bowl, saving marinade. Pour melted butter over chicken and toss until well coated. In batches, place wings evenly in one layer on bottom of air fryer basket. Cook at 375°F (190°C) for 14 minutes, flipping halfway through. Transfer chicken to a bowl and cover to keep warm. Repeat with next batch of wings. For the sauce, heat remaining marinade in a small pot. Bring to a boil, and then reduce heat and simmer for 10 minutes, stirring frequently, until thickened. Pour sauce over chicken wings and toss to coat. Makes 6 servings.

Combo air fryer: Cook for 22 minutes, flipping halfway through.

1 serving: 410 Calories; 16 g Total Fat (4 g Mono, 2 g Poly, 7 g Sat); 150 mg Cholesterol; 16 g Carbohydrate (0 g Fibre, 13 g Sugar); 50 g Protein; 720 mg Sodium

Crab Cakes

We had better success with these crab cakes in the dedicated air fryer rather than the combo unit. They did not crisp up well in the combo unit and did not hold their shape, but the model we used did not allow us to control the temperature. If your combo air fryer allows you to control the cooking temperature, this recipe should work fine. These cakes pair perfectly with the homemade remoulade sauce (see sidebar, below).

Olive oil	1 tbsp.	15 mL
Finely diced onion	1/4 cup	60 mL
Finely diced red pepper	1/4 cup	60 mL
Fresh bread crumbs	2/3 cup	175 mL
Mayonnaise	1/3 cup	75 mL
Finely chopped green onion	2 tsp.	10 mL
Dijon mustard	1 tsp.	5 mL
Chopped fresh dill	1 tsp.	5 mL
Large egg, beaten	1	1
Salt	1/2 tsp.	2 mL
Black pepper	1/4 tsp.	1 mL
Crabmeat	1 lb.	454 g
Panko bread crumbs	1 1/2 cups	375 mL

Heat olive oil in a small frying pan on medium until just hot. Add onion and red pepper and cook until vegetables start to soften but do not brown. Remove from heat and set aside to cool.

Combine onion mixture and next 8 ingredients in a large mixing bowl. Add crab meat and stir gently. Shape into 16 flat cakes. Press cakes into panko bread crumbs until evenly coated. Spray evenly with vegetable oil spray and transfer to air fryer basket, placing cakes as close together as possible. Cook at 400°F (200°C) until golden and crispy, about 12 minutes, flipping halfway through. Let cool for 5 minutes before serving. Makes 16 crab cakes.

Combo air fryer: Cook for 18 to 20 minutes, flipping halfway through.

1 crab cake: 110 Calories; 5 g Total Fat (3 g Mono, 1.5 g Poly, 0.5 g Sat); 40 mg Cholesterol; 8 g Carbohydrate (0 g Fibre, 0 g Sugar); 8 g Protein; 270 mg Sodium

〰 To make remoulade sauce, combine 1 cup (250 mL) of mayonnaise with 2 tbsp. (30 mL) of finely diced onions, 2 tbsp. (30 mL) gherkins, 1 tbsp. (15 mL) of grainy mustard, 1 tbsp. (15 mL) hot sauce and 1 tbsp. (15 mL) chopped parsley. Mix in 1/2 tbsp. (7 mL) of chopped capers and 1/2 tbsp. (7 mL) lemon juice, and salt and pepper to taste. Et Voilà! Remoulade sauce!

Jalapeño Poppers

For spicier poppers, leave some of the seeds in the jalapeños and replace the plain kettle potato chips with jalapeño-flavoured chips. If you need to cut the heat a little, serve your poppers with Ranch Dip (see p. 166).

Cream cheese, whipped	8 oz.	225 g
Grated Cheddar cheese	1 cup	250 mL
Bacon, cooked and crumbled	1/4 cup	60 mL
Garlic powder	1 tsp.	5 mL
Salt	1/2 tsp.	2 mL
Jalapeño pepper, halved, seeds and ribs removed (see Tip, page 28)	10	10
Crushed plain kettle potato chips	1/2 cup	125 mL

Combine first 5 ingredients in a large bowl. Spoon into jalapeño pepper halves (see Tip, below). Top with crushed potato chips. Spray with vegetable oil spray and cook at 350°F (175°C) until tops are crispy and jalapeños are tender, about 8 to 9 minutes. Remove from air fryer and set aside to cool for 3 minutes before serving. Makes 20 poppers.

Combo air fryer: Cook for 12 minutes, flipping halfway through.

2 poppers: 190 Calories; 15 g Total Fat (3.5 g Mono, 0.5 g Poly, 8 g Sat); 40 mg Cholesterol; 7 g Carbohydrate (1 g Fibre, 2 g Sugar); 6 g Protein; 310 mg Sodium

Tip: A simple way to fill the peppers is to scoop the cream cheese mixture into a resealable freezer bag. Seal the bag and snip an end off one corner. Pipe the cream cheese mixture into the jalapeño halves.

Spanakopita

This recipe takes a little planning ahead but is so worth it! Take the spinach and phyllo pastry out of the freezer the night before and let them thaw in the fridge. Make sure you have a bowl under the spinach in case it leaks as it thaws.

Butter, softened	3/4 cup	175mL
Olive oil	2 tbsp.	30 mL
Medium yellow onion, chopped	1/2	1/2
Salt	1/2 tsp.	2 mL
Packages of frozen spinach, thawed and squeezed dry (10 oz., 283 g, each)	2	2
Crumbled feta cheese	1 cup	250 mL
Chopped fresh dill	2 tbsp.	30 mL
Large egg	1	1
Dried thyme	1 tsp.	5 mL
Phyllo pastry sheets, thawed	10	10

Heat butter in a small saucepan on low heat until melted.

Heat olive oil in a medium frying pan on medium. Add onion and cook until caramelized, about 10 minutes. Stir in salt and set aside to cool.

Combine spinach, feta, dill, egg, thyme and onion in a large bowl.

On a clean work surface cut phyllo pastry into 4 inch (10 cm) wide strips widthwise and lay on top of each other. Cover pastry with a damp towel to prevent it from drying out. Lay one pastry strip on work surface and brush with butter. Top with a second pastry strip and brush with butter. Add 1 tbsp. (15 mL) filling and fold over into triangles, brushing with butter after each fold. Repeat with remaining pastry and filling. Transfer to air fryer tray leaving space between each piece. Cook at 325°F (160°C) for 10 minutes, then flip and cook for 2 minutes. Makes 20 spanakopita.

Combo air fryer: Cook on lowest rack for 10 minutes, then flip and cook for 4 minutes.

1 spanakopita: 140 Calories; 13 g Total Fat (3 g Mono, 0 g Poly, 7 g Sat); 45 mg Cholesterol; 3 g Carbohydrate (0 g Fibre, 0 g Sugar); 3 g Protein; 320 mg Sodium

Samosas

Serve these delicious veggie samosas with mint yogurt sauce (see sidebar) or your favourite mango chutney.

Ghee, or clarified butter	1 tbsp.	15 mL
Finely diced onions	1/2 cup	125 mL
Grated ginger root	1 tsp.	5 mL
Diced cooked potatoes	2 cups	500 mL
Garlic cloves, minced	3	3
Garam masala	1 tbsp.	15 mL
Finely chopped green chili (see Tip, page 28)	2 tsp.	10 mL
Chili powder	1 tsp.	5 mL
Turmeric	1 tsp.	5 mL
Salt	1 tsp.	5 mL
Fresh, or frozen thawed, green peas	1/3 cup	75 mL
Lemon juice	1 tbsp.	15 mL
Chopped fresh cilantro	2 tbsp.	30 mL
Samosa wrappers	16	16
Large egg whites, beaten	2	2

For the filling, heat ghee in a medium frying pan on medium. Add onion and ginger and cook for about 5 minutes until onion has softened.

Add next 7 ingredients. Cook, stirring, until fragrant about 2 minutes. Add peas and lemon juice. Cook until liquid has evaporated. Remove from heat and stir in cilantro. Set aside to cool.

Lay a samosa wrapper on work surface with shorter side facing toward you. Fold top left corner over to form a triangle. Fold triangle up to form a pocket. Brush egg white along outer edge and seal. Add 2 tbsp. (30 mL) filling into pocket. Brush top flap with egg white and fold over to seal. Set aside. Repeat with remaining dough and filling. Spray samosas evenly with vegetable oil spray and transfer to air fryer tray. Cook at 350°F (175°C) for 15 minutes, flipping halfway through. Makes 16 samosas.

1 samosa: 70 Calories; 1.5 g Total Fat (0 g Mono, 0 g Poly, 0.5 g Sat); 0 mg Cholesterol; 13 g Carbohydrate (0 g Fibre, 0 g Sugar); 2 g Protein; 210 mg Sodium

To make yogurt mint sauce, combine 1 cup (250 mL) plain Greek yogurt, 1 tbsp. (15 mL) mayonnaise, 2 tbsp. lemon juice, 3 tbsp. (45 mL) chopped fresh mint, 4 minced garlic cloves and 2 tbsp. (30 mL) chopped fresh parsley. Let stand for about 20 minutes before serving.

Sweet Potato Nachos

An innovative take on traditional nachos. Thinly sliced sweet potatoes, cooked to crispy perfection in the air fryer, take the place of tortilla chips with fantastic results. Be sure to serve plenty of salsa and sour cream on the side!

Large sweet potatoes, cut into 1/8 inch (3 mm) slices	2	2
Olive oil	1 tbsp.	15 mL
Taco seasoning	2 tbsp.	30 mL
Grated mozzarella cheese	1 1/2 cups	375mL
Grated old Cheddar cheese	1 1/2 cups	375mL
Green onion, thinly sliced diagonally	4	4
Red onion, thinly sliced	1/2	1/2
Shredded lettuce	1 cup	250 mL
Small tomato, chopped	1	1
Thinly sliced jalapeño pepper, seeds and ribs removed (see Tip, below)	1	1
Radishes, thinly sliced	6	6
Chopped fresh cilantro	1 tbsp.	15 mL

Combine first 3 ingredients in a large bowl and toss until well combined. Cook at 400°F (200°C) for 20 minutes, flipping halfway through.

Combine next 4 ingredients in a medium bowl. Sprinkle over nachos and cook for 12 minutes.

Sprinkle with remaining 5 ingredients and serve immediately. Makes 4 servings.

Combo air fryer: Cook sweet potatoes for 12 minutes, then flip and cook for 15 minutes. Sprinkle with cheese mixture and cook for 12 minutes.

1 serving: 450 Calories; 26 g Total Fat (7 g Mono, 1 g Poly, 15 g Sat); 75 mg Cholesterol; 31 g Carbohydrate (5 g Fibre, 7 g Sugar); 21 g Protein; 960 mg Sodium

Tip: Hot peppers contain capsaicin in the seeds and ribs. Removing the seeds will reduce the heat. Wear rubber gloves when handling hot peppers and avoid touching your eyes, Wash your hands well afterwards.

Sausage and Hash Brown Cups

Cheese, hash browns, sausage and egg with chunks of green pepper for a little splash of colour—what more could you ask for in a breakfast snack? Make sure you do not open the air fryer door to peek while the cups are cooking, or your eggs cups might collapse.

Cooking oil	2 tsp.	10 mL
Breakfast sausage, sliced	1 cup	250 mL
Chopped green pepper	1/2 cup	125 mL
Chopped onion	1/4 cup	60 mL
Frozen hash brown potatoes	2 cups	500 mL
Large eggs	4	4
Water	1/4 cup	60 mL
Salt	1 tsp.	5 mL
Black pepper	1/2 tsp.	2 mL
Grated medium Cheddar cheese	1/4 cup	60 mL
Grated partly skimmed mozzarella cheese	1/4 cup	60 mL
Grated medium Cheddar cheese	1/4 cup	60 mL
Grated partly skimmed mozzarella cheese	1/4 cup	60 mL
Chopped fresh parsley	2 tbsp.	30 mL

In a medium frying pan, heat oil on medium. Add next 3 ingredients and cook for 5 to 10 minutes, stirring often, until sausage is crisp. Add hash browns and cook for 5 minutes, stirring occasionally. Remove from heat.

Beat next 4 ingredients in a small bowl. Stir in first amounts of cheeses. Pour egg mixture over hash brown mixture. Stir until well combined. Scoop hash brown mixture into 4 greased 1 cup (250 mL) ramekins. Cook at 350°F (175°C), without opening air fryer door, until hash browns are cooked through and knife comes out clean, about 11 minutes.

Add remaining cheese and cook for 2 minutes. Remove ramekins from air fryer and let stand for 5 minutes to cool. Top with parsley and serve. Makes 4 cups.

Combo air fryer: Cook for 10 minutes, without opening air fryer door. Add remaining cheese and cook for 2 minutes.

1 cup (250 mL): 365 Calories; 23 g Total Fat (9 g Mono, 2 g Poly, 10 g Sat); 140 mg Cholesterol; 26 g Carbohydrate (2 g Fibre, 3 g Sugar); 16 g Protein; 1020 mg Sodium

Ham and Veggie Frittata

The great thing about frittatas is their versatility. Feel free to change up the veggies, ham or cheese to suit your preferences. The air fryer turns this frittata a rich golden brown. Be careful not to overcook (see Tip, below).

Large eggs	5	5
Whipping cream	1/4 cup	60 mL
Diced white onion	1/2 cup	125 mL
Diced green onion	1/4 cup	60 mL
Diced asparagus	1/2 cup	125 mL
Diced fresh white mushrooms	3/4 cup	175 mL
Deli Black Forest ham slices, diced	5	5
Grated Parmesan cheese	2 tbsp.	30 mL
Grated old Cheddar cheese	1/2 cup	125 mL
Salt	1/4 tsp.	1 mL
Black pepper	1/4 tsp.	1 mL
Grated old Cheddar cheese	2 tbsp.	30 mL
Chopped fresh parsley	1 tbsp.	15 mL
Olive oil, optional	1 tbsp.	15 mL

In a large bowl, whisk together eggs and cream.

Add next 9 ingredients and stir well. Line a deep 8 inch (20 cm) baking pan with parchment paper and spray lightly with vegetable oil spray. Pour egg mixture into baking pan and cook at 360°F (180°C) for 22 minutes.

Sprinkle frittata with remaining Cheddar and cook for 2 minutes. Transfer to a cutting board and cut into pizza-like slices. Drizzle with olive oil, if using, and garnish with chopped parsley. Makes 4 servings.

Combo air fryer: Cook for 24 minutes. Sprinkle with remaining cheese and cook for 10 minutes.

1 serving: 280 Calories; 21 g Total Fat (8 g Mono, 1.5 g Poly, 10 g Sat); 310 mg Cholesterol; 5 g Carbohydrate (1 g Fibre, 3 g Sugar); 17 g Protein; 540 mg Sodium

Tip: To check for doneness, insert a wooden pick in centre, like you would a cake. If the pick comes out clean, the frittata is cooked. Alternatively, give the frittata a little shake; if it is wobbly, it needs more time.

Breakfast Pockets

These handy little pockets can be stored in the fridge for up to five days, if they last that long! When you are ready to eat, just heat them in the microwave or toaster oven until they are warmed through.

All-purpose flour	1 1/2 cups	375 mL
Natural wheat bran	2/3 cup	150 mL
Granulated sugar	1 tsp.	5 mL
Salt	1/4 tsp.	1 mL
Instant yeast	1 1/4 tsp.	6 mL
Warm water	2/3 cup	150 mL
Fancy (mild) molasses	2 tbsp.	30 mL
Cooking oil	2 tbsp.	30 mL
Bacon slices, diced	6	6
Chopped onion	1/2 cup	125 mL
Large eggs, fork-beaten	6	6
Water	3 tbsp.	45 mL
Salt	1/2 tsp.	2 mL
Pepper, to taste		
Hash brown potatoes	1 cup	250 mL
Ketchup	1/3 cup	75 mL
Grated part-skim mozzarella cheese (about 3 oz., 85 g)	1/2 cup	125 mL
Grated Havarti cheese (about 3 oz. 85 g)	1/2 cup	125 mL
Large egg, fork beaten	1	1
Water	1 tbsp.	15 mL

Combine first 5 ingredients in a large bowl. Add next 3 ingredients. Mix well until dough leaves sides of bowl. Turn out onto a lightly floured surface. Knead for 5 to 8 minutes until smooth and elastic.

Place dough in a greased bowl, turning once to grease top. Cover with a tea towel. Let stand in oven with light on and door closed for about 1 hour until doubled in size. Punch dough down. Split into 8 individual balls. Roll each out to about an 8 inch (20 cm) round. Set aside.

Sauté bacon and onion in frying pan until bacon is golden and onion is soft. Drain well.

Add eggs, water, salt and pepper. Heat, stirring, until egg is half cooked. Add hash browns and cook, stirring, for 1 minute until egg is cooked. Spread ketchup over individual crusts, using 2 tsp. (10 mL) each. Spoon egg mixture over half of each round.

Toss both cheeses together in a small bowl. Sprinkle over filling.

Beat egg and water together. Brush edges of round with egg wash and fold dough over filling. Press down edges with a fork. Brush pocket with egg wash and cut slits in top. Transfer 2 pockets to air fryer basket sprayed with vegetable oil spray. Cook at 360°F (180°C) until golden brown, about 20 minutes, flipping halfway through. Repeat with remaining pockets. Makes 8 pockets.

Combo air fryer: Cook for 20 minutes, flipping halfway through.

1 pocket: 450 Calories; 27 g Total Fat (11 g Mono, 3.5 g Poly, 9 g Sat); 220 mg Cholesterol; 34 g Carbohydrate (3 g Fibre, 8 g Sugar); 16 g Protein; 670 mg Sodium

Potato Pancakes

This is another recipe that worked better in the dedicated air fryer than the combo unit. With the combo air fryer, we had difficulty achieving the desired texture, though the pancakes were still tasty. These pancakes are great topped with sour cream or sauteed apples, or if you ae feeling really indulgent, bacon and a fried or poached egg. Or go really fancy and top with caviar and crème fraiche.

Peeled, grated potatoes	4 cups	1 L
Medium onion, grated	1	1
Large eggs, beaten	2	2
All-purpose flour	3/4 cup	175 mL
Chopped chives	3 tbsp.	45 mL
Salt	1 1/2 tsp.	7 mL
Garlic powder	1 tsp.	5 mL
Black pepper	1/2 tsp.	2 mL
Sour cream or crème fraiche	1 cup	250 mL
Thinly sliced green onions	2 tbsp.	30 mL

Squeeze excess water from grated potatoes and drain well. Place in a large bowl.

Add next 7 ingredients and stir well. Form into 8 pancakes and spray evenly with vegetable oil spray. Place 4 pancakes in air fryer basket and cook at 375°F (190°C) until browned and crispy, about 14 minutes, flipping halfway through. Transfer to a plate and cover to keep warm. Repeat with remaining potato pancakes.

Serve with sour cream and sprinkle with green onions. Makes 8 pancakes.

Combo air fryer: Cook for 22 minutes, turning halfway through.

1 pancake: 200 Calories; 7 g Total Fat (2 g Mono, 0 g Poly, 4 g Sat); 65 mg Cholesterol; 29 g Carbohydrate (2 g Fibre, 4 g Sugar); 5 g Protein; 480 mg Sodium

Dutch Baby with Berry Compote

The air fryer does an amazing job of making this dish rise up nice and fluffy. No peeking while it cooks if you don't want it to fall! We've paired it with a special homemade mixed-berry compote, but it is also a delicious drizzled with maple syrup.

All-purpose flour	1/2 cup	125 mL
Salt	1/2 tsp.	2 mL
Large eggs	2	2
Milk	1/2 cup	125 mL
Butter, melted	2 tbsp.	30 mL
Butter	2 tbsp.	30 mL
Orange juice	3 tbsp.	45 mL
Icing (confectioner's) sugar	1/4 cup	60 mL
Strawberries, quartered	1 cup	250 mL
Raspberries	1 cup	250 mL
Blueberries	1/2 cup	125 mL
Blackberries	1/2 cup	125 mL
Whipped cream	1 cup	250 mL

Combine flour and salt in a small bowl.

Blend eggs in a blender on low speed. Add flour mixture and milk alternately in 6 additions. Blend until smooth. Add melted butter and blend.

Add remaining butter to 8 or 9 inch (20 or 23 cm) pan and heat in air fryer at 350°F (175°C) for 2 minutes. Carefully brush butter around pan, including sides. Re-blend Dutch baby mixture for 10 seconds. Pour batter into pan and cook, without opening air fryer door, until golden brown around edges and cooked through, about 10 minutes. Let cool for 5 minutes before serving.

For the compote, whisk together orange juice and icing sugar in a medium saucepan on medium heat. Bring to a boil, then reduce heat to a simmer and stir in berries. Cook for 5 to 6 minutes, stirring occasionally, until berries release their juice. Remove from heat to cool slightly.

Top Dutch baby with multi-berry compote and whipped cream. Makes 4 servings.

Combo air fryer: Cook for 12 minutes without opening air fryer door.

1 serving: 320 Calories; 22 g Total Fat (6 g Mono, 1 g Poly, 13 g Sat); 65 mg Cholesterol; 31 g Carbohydrate (5 g Fibre, 12 g Sugar); 3 g Protein; 150 mg Sodium

Raspberry White Chocolate Scones

This recipe works much better in a dedicated air fryer than a combo unit with a fixed air frying temperature. In our combo air fryer, the scones browned too much on top and were still a bit doughy inside. In the dedicated air fryer, these were scone perfection—rich and buttery with just the right amount of sweet from the white chocolate and raspberries. We couldn't stop eating them!

All-purpose flour	2 1/4 cups	550 mL
Granulated sugar	1/4 cup	60 mL
Baking powder	1 tbsp.	15 mL
Salt	1/2 tsp.	2 mL
Cold butter, cut up	1/2 cup	125 mL
Buttermilk (see Tip, below)	1 cup	250 mL
Chopped white chocolate	2/3 cup	175 mL
Fresh raspberries	1 cup	250 mL

Combine first 4 ingredients in a medium bowl. Cut butter into flour mixture until mixture resembles coarse crumbs.

Stir in buttermilk and white chocolate until just combined. Turn out onto a lightly flour surface and knead gently 3 or 4 times. Divide dough into 2 portions. Place 1 portion on a greased baking sheet and pat out dough to a 9 inch (23 cm) round.

Scatter half of raspberries over dough. Pat out remaining dough portion, place over raspberries and press down gently. Scatter remaining raspberries over top and press down gently against the raspberries. Cut dough carefully into 8 wedges. Bake at 365°F (180°C) until a wooden pick inserted in center comes out clean, about 8 to 10 minutes. Let cool for 5 minutes before serving. Makes 8 scones.

Combo air fryer: Cook for 10 to 12 minutes on lowest rack.

1 scone: 370 Calories; 18 g Total Fat (3 g Mono, .5 g Poly, 12 g Sat); 35 mg Cholesterol; 49 g Carbohydrate (2 g Fibre, 16 g Sugar); 4 g Protein; 380 mg Sodium

Tip: If you do not have buttermilk on hand, substitute soured milk instead. To make soured milk, pour 1 tbsp. (15 mL) white vinegar or lemon juice into a 1 cup (250 mL) liquid measure. Add enough milk to make 1 cup (250 mL). Stir. Let stand for 1 minute.

Sheet Pan Breakfast

Nothing beats the convenience and simplicity of a sheet pan breakfast when you crave a hearty meal. This dish smells fantastic as it is cooking. The aroma will lure even the soundest sleeper out of bed!

Baby potatoes, cut in half or quarters	1 1/2 lbs.	680 g
Large red pepper, chopped	1	1
Large yellow pepper, chopped	1	1
Maple syrup	1 tbsp.	15 mL
Olive oil	2 tbsp.	30 mL
Garlic powder	2 tsp.	10 mL
Salt	1 tsp.	5 mL
Black pepper	1 tsp.	5 mL
Cayenne powder	1/2 tsp.	2 mL
Breakfast sausage links	12	12
Maple syrup	1 tbsp.	15 mL

In a large bowl, toss baby potatoes, peppers, first amount of maple syrup and olive oil together. Add seasonings and mix well so seasonings are evenly distributed.

Transfer potato mixture to air fryer basket and add sausages. Cook at 400°F (200°C) until potatoes are crispy and sausages have cooked through, about 17 minutes, stirring halfway through.

Transfer to a serving platter and drizzle with remaining maple syrup. Stir gently and serve. Makes 4 servings.

Combo air fryer: Cook for 25 minutes, stirring halfway through.

1 serving: 430 Calories; 21 g Total Fat (4.5 g Mono, 1 g Poly, 6 g Sat); 35 mg Cholesterol; 44 g Carbohydrate (4 g Fibre, 7 g Sugar); 16 g Protein; 1210 mg Sodium

Sheet Pan Beef Fajitas

The recipe makes a large batch of fajitas. If you are using a combo air fryer, depending on the size or your unit, you may need to cook this meal in batches, or cut the recipe in half if you don't need so many servings.

Brown sugar	2 tbsp.	30 mL
Kosher salt	1 tsp.	5 mL
Chili powder	1 tbsp.	15 mL
Ground cumin	1/2 tsp.	2 mL
Garlic powder	1/2 tsp.	2 mL
Onion powder	1/2 tsp.	2 mL
Dried oregano	1/2 tsp.	2 mL
Smoked paprika	1/2 tsp.	2 mL
Large red or orange pepper, sliced	1	1
Large green pepper, sliced	1	1
Large red onion, sliced	1	1
Top sirloin steak, sliced into 1/2 inch (12 mm) strips	1 1/2 lbs.	680 g
Olive oil	2 tbsp.	30 mL
Flour tortillas (9 inch, 23 cm, in diameter)	12	12
Salsa	1 cup	250 mL
Sour cream	1/2 cup	125 mL
Chopped fresh cilantro	2 tbsp.	30 mL

Combine first 8 ingredients together in a small bowl.

In a large bowl combine vegetables and steak strips. Drizzle with oil and add spice mixture. Toss until well combined. Spread out evenly on air fryer basket and cook at 400°F (200°C) for 12 minutes, shaking basket halfway through.

To assemble fajitas, place some of beef mixture on a warm tortilla shell and top with salsa, sour cream and cilantro. Makes 6 servings.

Combo air fryer: Cook for 20 minutes, stirring halfway through. May need to be cooked in batches, depending on the size of your air fryer.

1 serving: 490 Calories; 20 g Total Fat (9 g Mono, 2 g Poly, 7 g Sat); 65 mg Cholesterol; 39 g Carbohydrate (7 g Fibre, 11 g Sugar); 27 g Protein; 850 mg Sodium

Pork Satay Sheet Pan Dinner

If you want this to be a true sheet pan meal, you can skip the homemade satay sauce and use your favourite store-bought brand instead, but we think our sauce is worth the extra step!

Smooth peanut butter	1/2 cup	125 mL
Coconut milk	1/2 cup	125 mL
Brown sugar	1/4 cup	60 mL
Garlic cloves, minced	3	3
Low sodium soy sauce	2 tbsp.	30 mL
Fresh lime juice	1 tbsp.	15 mL
Fresh ginger root, grated	2 tsp.	10 mL
Dried crushed chilies	1 tsp.	5 mL
Turmeric	1/4 tsp.	60 mL
Pork tenderloin, cut into 1 inch (2.5 cm) pieces	1 lbs.	454 g
Yams, cut into 1 inch (2.5 cm) pieces	2 cups	500 g
Frozen cauliflower florets	3 cups	750 g
Olive oil	2 tsp.	10 mL
Chopped fresh cilantro	3 tbsp.	45 mL

For the sauce, carefully whisk first 9 ingredients together in a medium pot on medium heat. Bring to a boil, and then reduce heat and simmer for 6 to 8 minutes, stirring frequently, to combine flavours. Remove from heat.

Toss next 4 ingredients together in a large bowl. Add 1/2 cup (125 mL) satay sauce and stir until pork and vegetables are evenly coated. Spread pork mixture evenly in air fryer basket and cook at 400°F (200°C) until pork is cooked through, about 18 minutes, stirring or shaking basket halfway through.

Transfer to a serving platter and toss with remaining sauce to coat evenly. Sprinkle with cilantro. Makes 4 servings.

Combo air fryer: Cook for 26 minutes, stirring or shaking the basket a third and again two-thirds of the way through.

1 serving: 560 Calories; 32 g Total Fat (4.5 g Mono, 1 g Poly, 12 g Sat); 75 mg Cholesterol; 41 g Carbohydrate (6 g Fibre, 21 g Sugar); 34 g Protein; 570 mg Sodium

Sheet Pan Chicken Milanese

Although this is technically a sheet pan recipe, as it is cooked all on one pan, for best results you should cook the chicken first, then remove it from the air fryer and cook the veggies separately so the tomatoes don't release their juices onto the chicken and make it soggy.

Boneless, skinless chicken breasts (about 6 oz., 170 g each)	2	2
Salt	1 tsp.	5 mL
Black pepper	1 tsp.	5 mL
All-purpose flour	1/2 cup	125 mL
Large eggs, fork-beaten	2	2
Panko bread crumbs	1/3 cup	75 mL
Grated Parmesan cheese	1/4 cup	60 mL
Garlic powder	1 tsp	5 mL
Tomatoes on the vine, cut into quarters	5	5
Fresh asparagus spears, trimmed of tough ends	18	18
Olive oil	3 tbsp.	45 mL
Salt	1 tsp.	5 mL
Black pepper	1/2 tsp.	2 mL
Medium shallot, thinly sliced	1	1
Lemon juice	1 tsp.	5 mL
Arugula	2 cups	500 mL
Chopped fresh parsley, for garnish		
Chopped fresh basil, for garnish		
Parmesan cheese, for garnish		

Place chicken between 2 sheets of plastic wrap. Pound with a mallet or rolling pin until flattened. Sprinkle chicken with salt and pepper on both sides.

Place flour in a shallow dish. Whisk together eggs and place in a second shallow dish. Combine bread crumbs, Parmesan and garlic powder in a third shallow dish. Coat each chicken breast in flour on both sides, then dip in egg and then into bread crumbs. Spray both sides with vegetable oil spray. Cook at 400°F (200°C) for 12 minutes, flipping halfway through. Transfer to a plate and cover with foil to keep warm.

In a small bowl, toss tomatoes, asparagus, olive oil, salt, pepper, shallots and lemon juice. Cook at 350°F (175°C) for 12 minutes, stirring halfway through.

Place arugula on a serving platter and top with tomato and asparagus. Add chicken on top and garnish with chopped parsley and basil. Makes 2 servings.

Combo air fryer: Cook chicken for 16 minutes, flipping halfway through. Cook asparagus and tomatoes for 20 minutes, stirring halfway through.

1 serving: 740 Calories; 32 g Total Fat (18 g Mono, 4 g Poly, 7 g Sat); 320 mg Cholesterol; 53 g Carbohydrate (9 g Fibre, 12 g Sugar); 61 g Protein; 1580 mg Sodium

Butternut Squash Ravioli Sheet Pan

In this dish we used skinny spears of asparagus; if your asparagus spears are thicker, you may have to adjust the amount and cooking time accordingly.

Olive oil	1/4 cup	60 mL
Brussel sprouts, halved	1 cup	250 mL
Medium zucchini, sliced into 1 inch (2.5 cm) circles	1	1
Fresh asparagus spears, trimmed of tough ends	36	36
Medium red pepper, chopped	1	1
Package of butternut squash ravioli (8 oz., 250 g)	1	1
Garlic cloves, crushed	4	4
Chopped fresh parsley	2 tbsp.	30 mL
Dried crushed chilies	1 tsp.	5 mL
Salt	1/2 tsp.	2 mL
Black pepper	1 tbsp.	15 mL
Whipping cream	1 tbsp.	15 mL
Finely grated Parmesan cheese	1/4 cup	60 mL

Combine all 13 ingredients in a large bowl, mixing well. Let stand for 10 minutes to allow flavours to blend. Cook at 325°F (160°C) for 12 minutes. Let cool for 5 minutes before serving. Makes 4 servings.

Combo air fryer: Cook for 12 minutes.

1 serving: 330 Calories; 18 g Total Fat (11 g Mono, 1.5 g Poly, 4.5 g Sat); 20 mg Cholesterol; 35 g Carbohydrate (5 g Fibre, 8 g Sugar); 10 g Protein; 730 mg Sodium

Pot Roast

Forget low and slow for this pot roast. With the air fryer, this dish can be on the table in less than 45 minutes, and it is every bit as tender and delicious as a roast slow cooked in the oven. Be sure to let the meat stand for at least 5 minutes before slicing. Garnish with fresh herbs for an attractive presentation.

Salt	1 tsp.	5 mL
Brown sugar	2 tbsp.	30 mL
Black pepper	1 tbsp.	15 mL
Dried thyme	2 tbsp.	30 mL
Fresh rosemary, chopped	2 tbsp.	30 mL
Paprika	1 tsp.	5 mL
Diced jalapeño pepper, seeds and ribs removed (see Tip, page 28)	1	1
Sirloin tip roast	1 3/4 lb.	760 g
Olive oil	2 tbsp.	30 mL
Medium yellow onion, cut into 8 wedges	2	2
Medium carrots, cut into 4 pieces each	4	4
Medium celery stalks, cut into 4 pieces each	4	4

Combine salt, brown sugar, pepper, thyme, rosemary, paprika, and jalapeño on a shallow plate. Brush beef with oil and coat with spice mixture, rubbing spice mix in with your hands. Place on air fryer tray.

Toss vegetables on same plate so veggies are coated with spice mixture. Place on tray with beef. Cook at 400°F (200°C) for 10 minutes, then reduce heat to 360°F (180°C) and cook for 6 minutes. Flip beef over. Remove onions from tray and set aside, covered to keep warm. Cook beef and remaining vegetables for 8 minutes. Let meat stand for 5 minutes before slicing. Return onions to tray and stir. Makes 4 servings.

Combo air fryer: Cook for 40 minutes.

1 serving: 580 Calories; 36 g Total Fat (19 g Mono, 2 g Poly, 13 g Sat); 130 mg Cholesterol; 21 g Carbohydrate (4 g Fibre, 12 g Sugar); 40 g Protein; 790 mg Sodiuml

Fast Fried Steak with Shallot Butter

Serve this steak with fries for the classic brasserie dish "steak frites." The cooking time can vary depending on the thickness of your steak, so watch it carefully.

Rib eye steak (about 12 oz., 340 g, and 3/4 inch, 2 cm, thick)	1	1
Butter, softened	1/4 cup	60 mL
Minced shallots	1 tbsp.	15 mL
Chopped fresh parsley	1 tbsp.	15 mL
Lemon juice	1 tsp.	5 mL
White pepper	1/4 tsp.	1 mL
Dried rosemary	2 tsp.	10 mL
Garlic powder	1 tsp.	5 mL
Salt	1 tsp.	5 mL
Black pepper	1/2 tsp.	2 mL

Allow steak to come to room temperature.

For the shallot butter, beat next 5 ingredients together in a small bowl. Transfer to a piece of parchment or wax paper and roll into a cylinder shape, about 1 inch (2.5 cm) wide. Chill until firm.

Combine next 4 ingredients in a small bowl. Spray steak with vegetable oil spray and season with spice mixture on both sides. Cook at 400°F (200°C) for 8 minutes, flipping halfway through, until internal temperature reaches 130° to 135°F (55° to 57°C) for medium-rare doneness. Remove steak from air fryer and let stand for at least 5 minutes. Cut steak half. Slice compound butter into 1/4 inch (6 mm) thick slices and place on top of each half to serve. Makes 2 servings.

Combo air fryer: Cook for 12 minutes, flipping halfway through.

1 serving: 660 Calories; 58 g Total Fat (6 g Mono, 1 g Poly, 28 g Sat); 195 mg Cholesterol; 5 g Carbohydrate (0 g Fibre, 0 g Sugar); 33 g Protein; 1420 mg Sodium

Stuffed Blueberry Burger

Stilton cheese and blueberries are mixed right into the beef, which encloses a pocket of gooey provolone cheese. You will love every savoury, cheesy bite!

Ingredient	Imperial	Metric
Finely chopped onions	1/2 cup	125 mL
Chopped frozen blueberries	1/3 cup	75 mL
Beef broth	1/4 cup	60 mL
Fine dry bread crumbs (see Tip, page 134)	1/4 cup	60 mL
Garlic cloves, minced	3	3
Salt	1 tsp.	5 mL
Black pepper	1/2 tsp.	2 mL
Lean ground beef	1 lb.	454 g
Crumbled Stilton cheese	1/4 cup	60 mL
Grated provolone cheese	1/2 cup	125 mL
Hamburger buns	4	4
Aioli	1/2 cup	125 mL
Lettuce leaf	4	4
Tomato slices	4	4
Red onion slices	4	4

Combine first 7 ingredients in a large bowl.

Add beef and Stilton cheese. Mix until just combined. Shape into 4 patties. Remove 3 tbsp. (45 mL) of meat from center of each patty. Add 2 tbsp. (30 mL) of provolone to center of each burger and cover with remaining beef mixture. Spray burgers evenly with vegetable oil spray. Cook at 375°F (190°C) for 12 minutes, flipping halfway through. Let stand for 5 minutes before serving.

Spread bottom bun with 2 tbsp. (30 mL) aioli and top with lettuce leaf. Add burger and top with tomatoes, red onion slices, and bun top. Makes 4 burgers.

Combo air fryer: Cook for 15 minutes, flipping halfway through.

1 burger: 700 Calories; 46 g Total Fat (9 g Mono, 20 g Poly, 15 g Sat); 125 mg Cholesterol; 28 g Carbohydrate (2 g Fibre, 6 g Sugar); 33 g Protein; 1190 mg Sodium

Mini Stuffed Meatloaves

Cute individual-sized meatloaves stuffed with a rich spinach and provolone filling. Make sure there are no seams in your ground beef mixture before you put it in the air fryer or the cheese will leak out during cooking. Serve with mashed potatoes and steamed or roasted carrots.

Butter	1 tbsp.	15 mL
Finely chopped onions	1/2 cup	125 mL
Garlic cloves, minced	2	2
Ground beef	1 lb.	454 g
Panko bread crumbs	1/2 cup	125 mL
Beef broth	1/4 cup	60 mL
Large egg, beaten	2	2
Worcestershire sauce	2 tsp.	10 mL
Dry mustard powder	1 tsp.	5 mL
Salt	1 tsp.	5 mL
Black pepper	1/2 tsp.	2 mL
Baby spinach, blanched	2 cups	500 mL
Grated provolone cheese	2/3 cup	175 mL
Ketchup	1/4 cup	60 mL
Tomato paste	2 tbsp.	30 mL
Apple cider vinegar	2 tbsp.	30 mL
Brown sugar	2 tbsp.	30 mL
Worcestershire sauce	1 tbsp.	15 mL
Garlic powder	1/2 tsp.	2 mL
Cayenne powder	1/4 tsp.	1 mL

Melt butter in a small frying pan on medium, melt butter heat. Add onion and cook for 5 minutes, stirring occasionally, until onion begins to soften. Add garlic and cook, stirring, until fragrant, about 2 minutes. Remove from heat.

Combine ground beef and next 7 ingredients in a large bowl. Mix well. Add onion mixture and mix until well combined.

In a small bowl combine spinach and provolone cheese. Divide ground beef mixture into 6 equal mini loaves. Remove top third of each loaf. Make a depression in middle of loaves and fill with spinach mixture. Replace top of each mini loaf, smoothing to ensure there are no seams. Place loaves on a piece of parchment paper that will fit into air fryer.

For the glaze, whisk last 7 ingredients together in a medium bowl. Transfer parchment paper to air fryer basket. Brush a quarter of sauce onto loaves. Cook at 400°F (200°C) until internal temperature reaches 160°F (71°C), about 12 minutes. Brush meatloaf tops with sauce again and cook for 1 minute. Let stand for 5 minutes before serving. Serve with additional sauce on side. Makes 6 mini meatloaves.

Combo air fryer: Cook for 20 minutes, spinning the tray around halfway through. Brush with sauce and cook for 1 minute.

1 mini meatloaf: 325 Calories; 17 g Total Fat (6 g Mono, 0.5 g Poly, 8 g Sat); 130 mg Cholesterol; 15 g Carbohydrate (1 g Fibre, 9 g Sugar); 21 g Protein; 790 mg Sodium

Ginger Beef

The air fryer works its magic to cook up perfectly crispy ginger beef without the need for deep frying! Garnish your dish with thinly sliced carrot, peppers and green onion for an attractive presentation.

Cornstarch	3/4 cup	175 mL
Water, room temperature	1/2 cup	125 mL
Large eggs	2	2
Flank steak (or beef tenderloin)	1 lb.	454 g
Vegetable oil	2 tbsp.	30 mL
Medium yellow onion, thinly sliced	1	1
Large carrot, thinly sliced	1	1
Medium green pepper, thinly sliced	1	1
Medium red pepper, thinly sliced	1/2	1/2
Green onions, chopped	4	4
Tamari	2 tbsp.	30 mL
Mirin	1 tbsp.	15 mL
Sherry vinegar	1 tbsp.	15 mL
Brown sugar	1 tsp.	5 mL
Ginger paste	1 tbsp.	15 mL
Ginger root, peeled, thinly sliced	1 tbsp.	15 mL

In a medium bowl, whisk together cornstarch and water. Stir in eggs.

Slice beef into 1 inch (2.5 cm) thick slices and place in bowl with egg mixture. Let stand in refrigerator for 10 minutes to marinate.

Heat oil in a medium frying pan on medium-high. Add onion and cook for 3 minutes. Add carrots, green pepper, red pepper and green onion and cook for 5 minutes.

Add tamari, mirin, sherry vinegar, brown sugar, ginger paste and ginger root. Cook, stirring often, until slightly thickened, about 7 minutes. Stir in beef and toss to coat. Transfer to air fryer basket and cook at 400°F (200°C) for 6 minutes. Flip beef and cook for 8 minutes. Makes 4 servings.

Combo air fryer: Cook for 12 minutes, flipping beef halfway through.

1 serving: 430 Calories; 18 g Total Fat (7 g Mono, 3 g Poly, 6 g Sat); 150 mg Cholesterol; 34 g Carbohydrate (2 g Fibre, 7 g Sugar); 30 g Protein; 480 mg Sodium

Mini Moussaka

This recipe is long but sooooo worth the effort. Layers of potato, eggplant and zucchini are smothered with a savoury homemade meat sauce and creamy bechamel.

Large russet potatoes, peeled, thinly sliced in circles	2	2
Large eggplant, thinly sliced in circles	2	2
Large zucchini, thinly sliced into circles	1	1
Olive oil	1/4 cup	60 mL
Dried thyme	2 tbsp.	30 mL
Dried oregano	1 tbsp.	15 mL
Salt	2 tsp.	10 mL
Black pepper	1 tsp.	5 mL
Olive oil	3 tbsp.	45 mL
Medium yellow onion, diced	1	1
Garlic cloves, diced	2	2
Granulated sugar	1/2 tsp.	2 mL
Ground cinnamon	1 tsp.	5 mL
Ground nutmeg	1/2 tsp.	2 mL
Lean ground beef	2 cups	500 mL
Tomato paste	2 tbsp.	30 mL
Can of plum tomatoes (28 oz., 796 mL)	1	1
Chopped fresh basil	3/4 cup	175 mL
Salt	1 tsp.	5 mL
Black pepper	1 tsp.	5 mL
Unsalted butter, softened	1/2 cup	125 mL
All-purpose flour	1/2 cup	125 mL
Whole milk	3 cups	750 mL
Salt	1 tsp.	5 mL
Ground nutmeg	1/2 tsp.	2 mL
Grated Parmesan cheese	1/2 cup	125 mL
Egg yolks	3	3
Grated Parmesan cheese	1/4 cup	60 mL

Combine first 8 ingredients in a large bowl, tossing until vegetables are well coated. Cook at 400°F (200°C) for 18 minutes, in batches if necessary, flipping halfway through.

For the meat sauce, heat second amount of oil in a large saucepan on medium-high. Add next five ingredients and cook until onions are caramelized, about 7 minutes.

Add ground beef, and scramble-fry until no longer pink. Stir in tomato paste and cook for 2 minutes. Add tomatoes, breaking them up with a fork. Reduce heat to a simmer and cook for at least 30 minutes. Stir in chopped basil, salt and pepper.

For the bechamel, melt butter in a medium saucepan over medium heat. Whisk in flour until incorporated. Add milk 1/2 cup (125 mL) at a time, stirring continuously, until mixture is smooth and thickens enough to coat back of a spoon. Remove from heat and whisk in salt, nutmeg, Parmesan and egg yolks.

To assemble moussaka, layer potatoes, eggplant and zucchini in bottom of eight 2 cup (500 ml) ramekins. Stir 3 tbsp. (45 mL) bechamel into meat sauce and spread over vegetable layer. Top with bechamel and sprinkle with Parmesan. Cook until tops are bubbly and browned, about 18 minutes. Makes 8 mini moussaka.

Combo air fryer: Cook veggies for 18 minutes, flipping halfway through. Top with meat sauce and bechamel and cook for 18 minutes, until bubbly and browned.

1 moussaka: 590 Calories; 35 g Total Fat (15 g Mono, 2.5 g Poly, 14 g Sat); 160 mg Cholesterol; 46 g Carbohydrate (9 g Fibre, 14 g Sugar); 27 g Protein; 1650 mg Sodium

Jamaican Beef Patties

Enjoy a taste of the Caribbean with these delicious puff pastry pockets filled with curried ground beef. The air fryer turns the pastry a lovely golden brown but keep a close eye on your patties to be sure they do not get too dark.

Peanut oil	2 tbsp.	30 mL
Medium yellow onion, diced	1	1
Lean ground beef	1 1/2 lbs.	680 g
Dried thyme	2 tbsp.	30 mL
Green onions, chopped	4	4
Celery stick, diced	1	1
Curry powder	2 tbsp.	30 mL
Salt	1 tsp.	5 mL
Water	1 cup	250 mL
Package of puff pastry	1	1
(2 pre-rolled sheets, 450 g, per package)		
All-purpose flour, for dusting		
Large egg, fork-beaten	1	1
Water	1/4 cup	60 mL
Unsalted butter, melted	1 tbsp.	15 mL

Heat peanut oil in a medium frying pan on medium. Add onion and cook until softened, about 6 minutes. Add beef and mash with a hand masher until onion and beef are combined.

Add thyme, green onion, celery, curry powder and salt and cook until beef is almost browned, about 7 minutes.

Add first amount of water. There should be enough to just cover beef. Turn heat down and simmer for 40 to 50 minutes, stirring occasionally, until most of liquid has evaporated. Remove from heat and let stand for a few minutes to give mixture time to soak up remaining liquid.

Lay pastry on a clean work surface, dusting surface with flour if pastry sticks. Using a 6 inch (15 cm) circle cutter, cut 4 circles in each pastry sheet. Place 1/3 cup (75 mL) beef mixture to one side of circle. Fold dough over to enclose filling. Press a fork gently around outside edge. Repeat with remaining dough and filling.

Combine egg and remaining water. Brush both sides of patties with egg wash. Transfer to air fryer tray, leaving space between patties. Cook at 350°F (175°C) for 3 minutes.

Melt butter in a small microwave-safe bowl. Flip patties and brush tops with butter. Cook for 4 minutes. Makes 8 patties.

Combo air fryer. Cook for 6 minutes. Flip patties, brush with butter and cook for 6 more minutes.

1 patty: 720 Calories; 44 g Total Fat (7 g Mono, 1.5 g Poly, 20 g Sat); 110 mg Cholesterol; 51 g Carbohydrate (1 g Fibre, 1 g Sugar); 24 g Protein; 700 mg Sodium

Carne Asada

Carne asada, meaning "grilled meat" in Spanish, is a dish that originated in Mexico. As its name suggests, the steak in this dish is traditionally grilled, but the air fryer does a fantastic job with delicious results. These flavourful steak strips can be eaten as a main with a side of rice, or use them in tacos or burritos.

Orange juice	1/4 cup	60 mL
Chipotle peppers in adobe sauce, chopped	3 tbsp.	45 mL
White wine vinegar	2 tbsp.	30 mL
Garlic, cloves, minced	4	4
Chopped fresh cilantro	1 tbsp.	15 mL
Chili powder	1 tbsp.	15 mL
Vegetable oil	1 tbsp.	15 mL
Orange zest	2 tsp.	10 mL
Ground cumin	2 tsp.	10 mL
Salt	1 tsp.	5 mL
Flank steak	1 1/2 lbs.	680 g
Corn tortillas (6 inch, 15 cm, diameter)	12	12
Diced onions	1/2 cup	125 mL
Queso fresco	1/2 cup	125 mL
Chopped fresh pineapple, optional	1/2 cup	125 mL
Sliced avocado, optional	1	1
Chopped fresh cilantro	3 tbsp.	45 mL

Combine first 10 ingredients in a small bowl.

Place steak in a large resealable plastic bag. Add chipotle mixture, seal bag and turn to coat. Marinate in refrigerator for at least 2 and up to 4 hours. Remove steak. Drain chipotle mixture into a small saucepan. Boil gently for about 5 minutes, or until thickened. Place steak mixture in air fryer basket and cook at 400°F (200°C) for 12 minutes, stirring halfway through. Transfer steak to a cutting board and let stand for 10 minutes. Cut steak along grain and drizzle with reserved chipotle mixture.

Divide steak evenly amongst corn tortillas. Top with onions, pineapple, avocado slices, and fresh cilantro. Makes 12 servings.

Combo air fryer: Cook for 18 minutes, stirring halfway through.

1 serving: 190 Calories; 9 g Total Fat (4 g Mono, 1 g Poly, 2.5 g Sat); 25 mg Cholesterol; 15 g Carbohydrate (3 g Fibre, 1 g Sugar); 14 g Protein; 250 mg Sodium

Sweet Garlic Pork Tenderloin

This is a simple, yet a delicious way to prepare a pork tenderloin. The spice mix gives it a wonderful crust while the meat remains tender and juicy on the inside.

Pork tenderloins (1 lb., 454 g, each)	2	2
Brown sugar	2 tbsp.	30 mL
Smoked paprika	1 tbsp.	15 mL
Salt	1 tsp.	5 mL
Mustard powder	1 tsp.	5 mL
Garlic powder	1/2 tsp.	2 mL
Onion powder	1/4 tsp.	1 mL
Black pepper	1/4 tsp.	1 mL
Chili powder, optional	1/4 tsp.	1 mL

Cut each tenderloin in half so you have 4 pieces in total. Remove all excess fat. Spray with vegetable oil spray.

Combine next 8 ingredients in a small bowl. Rub mixture all over tenderloin pieces ensuring they are covered evenly. Transfer to air fryer basket and cook at 400°F (200°C) until meat reaches an internal temperature of 145° to 150°F (63° to 65°C), about 20 minutes, flipping halfway through. Remove from air fryer and let stand for 6 to 7 minutes before slicing. Makes 4 servings.

Combo air fryer: Cook for 24 minutes, flipping halfway through.

1 serving: 340 Calories; 13 g Total Fat (6 g Mono, 1.5 g Poly, 4.5 g Sat); 150 mg Cholesterol; 8 g Carbohydrate (0 g Fibre, 7 g Sugar); 47 g Protein; 700 mg Sodium

Crab-stuffed Pork Chops

These thick pork chops are stuffed with a cheesy crab filling and then drizzled with a rich buttery sauce. Decadent!

Butter	2 tbsp.	30 mL
Medium red onion	1/4	1/4
Medium yellow pepper, chopped	1	1
Can of crabmeat (4 1/4 oz., 120 g), drained	1	1
Chopped fresh parsley	2 tbsp.	30 mL
Chopped fresh basil	1 tbsp.	15 mL
Dry bread crumbs (see Tip, page 134)	2 tbsp.	30 mL
Large egg	1	1
Grated Edam cheese	1/2 cup	125 mL
Salt	1/2 tsp.	2 mL
Black pepper	1/2 tsp.	2 mL
Smoked paprika	1 tbsp.	15 mL
Cayenne pepper	1 tbsp.	15 mL
Chili powder	1 tbsp.	15 mL
Garlic powder	1 tbsp.	15 mL
Salt	1/2 tsp.	2 mL
Black pepper	1/2 tsp.	2 mL
Bone-in pork loin rib end chops, trimmed of fat (about 1 inch, 2.5 cm, thick each)	4	4
Butter	2 tbsp.	30 mL
Half and half cream	1 cup	250 mL
Garlic paste	1 tbsp.	15 mL
Grated Parmesan cheese	1/2 cup	125 mL
Chopped fresh parsley, for garnish		

For the stuffing, heat butter in a large frying pan on medium and cook onion and peppers for 5 to 6 minutes until softened. Transfer to a large bowl and set aside to cool.

Add next 8 ingredients. Mix well and set aside.

Combine next 6 ingredients in a small bowl. Cut a pocket into each pork chop. Stuff with crab mixture and secure with a toothpick. Sprinkle with spice mixture, making sure every part is coated. Cook at 400°F (200°C) for 16 minutes, flipping halfway through.

For the sauce, bring butter and cream to a low boil in a saucepan on medium-high. Add garlic paste and cook for 1 minute. Stir in Parmesan and simmer for 5 minutes. Pour over pork chops, and garnish with parsley. Makes 4 pork chops.

Combo air fryer: Cook for 10 minutes, then flip and cook for 8 minutes.

1 pork chop with sauce: 600 Calories; 41 g Total Fat (12 g Mono, 3 g Poly, 21 g Sat); 220 mg Cholesterol; 15 g Carbohydrate (3 g Fibre, 4 g Sugar); 40 g Protein; 170 mg Sodium

Pork Back Dry Ribs

Though conventional wisdom suggests that ribs are best when cooked low and slow, the air fryer does an admirable job in a fraction of the time. Perfect for those days when you just can't wait to dig in to a plate of home-cooked ribs! Serve with chili dipping sauce and fresh lime slices on the side.

Tamari	3 tbsp.	45 mL
White wine vinegar	2 tbsp.	30 mL
Sesame oil	1 1/2 tsp.	7 mL
Honey	2 tbsp.	30 mL
Chinese five-spice powder	1 tbsp.	15 mL
Garlic powder	1 tbsp.	15 mL
Ground ginger	1 tsp.	5 mL
Sweet-and-sour-cut pork ribs, individually cut, bone in	2.2 lbs.	1 kg
Green onions, thinly sliced, for garnish	2	2

Place first 7 ingredients in a large bowl and whisk until well combined.

Place pork in a large resealable freezer bag. Pour marinade into bag and seal, ensuring all air has been squeezed out of bag. Using both hands, squeeze bag to coat meat with marinade. Marinate in refrigerator for 6 hours to overnight, flipping bag over at halfway point. Cook at 400°F (200°C) for 18 minutes, flipping hallway through.

Sprinkle with green onion and serve. Makes 4 servings.

Combo air fryer: Cook for 40 minutes, flipping halfway through.

1 serving: 760 Calories; 59 g Total Fat (0.5 g Mono, 0.5 g Poly, 20 g Sat); 200 mg Cholesterol; 13 g Carbohydrate (2 g Fibre, 9 g Sugar); 39 g Protein; 960 mg Sodium

Sausage Lasagna Bites

Think of these little bites as deconstructed lasagna. They have all the usual lasagna goodness in an innovative package. The Italian sausage gives the bites an extra bit of oomph. We've used manicotti shells in place of lasagna noodles because they are easier to work with.

Olive oil	3 tbsp.	45 mL
White onion, chopped	1/2	1/2
Garlic cloves, chopped	4	4
Italian sausage, casings removed	3	3
Spicy Italian sausage, casings removed	2	2
Lean ground beef	2 cups	500 mL
Mushrooms, chopped	2 cups	500 mL
Celery ribs, chopped	2	2
Italian seasoning	1 tbsp.	15 mL
Salt	1 tsp.	5 mL
Dried oregano	1 tbsp.	15 mL
Tomato paste	6 tbsp.	90 mL
Water	1/4 cup	60 mL
Fresh Italian parsley, chopped	1 tbsp.	15 mL
Can of plum tomatoes (28 oz., 796 mL),	1	1
Dried crushed chilies	1/4 tsp.	1 mL
Beef broth	2 cups	500 mL
Olive oil	1 tsp.	5 mL
Spinach	2 cups	500 mL
Ricotta	1 cup	250 mL
Salt	1/2 tsp.	2 mL
Black pepper	1 tsp.	5 mL
Grated old Cheddar cheese	1/2 cup	125 mL
Finely grated Parmigiano Reggiano cheese	1/2 cup	125 mL
Cooked manicotti shells	8	8
Grated mozzarella cheese	1/2 cup	125 mL

For the meat sauce, heat first amount of olive oil in a large frying pan on medium-high. Add onion and cook, stirring often, until starting to soften. Add garlic, sausage and beef and cook until browned, about 10 minutes. Add mushrooms and cook for another 6 minutes. Reduce heat to medium. Add celery and Italian seasoning, salt and oregano and cook for about 5 minutes. Add tomato paste and cook for 4 minutes. Stir in water, parsley, tomatoes and dried chilies. Add beef broth and bring to a boil, then reduce heat and simmer for 1 hour, stirring occasionally.

For the filling, heat second amount of oil in a non-stick skillet on medium. Add spinach and cook, stirring often, until wilted. Combine next 5 ingredients in a large bowl. Add spinach and mix well. Stuff each shell with mixture and place in air fryer tray. Cook at 400°F (200°C) for 12 minutes.

Sprinkle with mozzarella and cook for 3 minutes. To serve, you can pour the meat sauce over the lasagna bites or spoon the sauce onto the plate and place bites on sauce. Makes 8 servings.

Combo air fryer: Cook for 12 minutes. Sprinkle with mozzarella and cook for 3 minutes.

1 serving: 610 Calories; 40 g Total Fat (15 g Mono, 2.5 g Poly, 15 g Sat); 105 mg Cholesterol; 25 g Carbohydrate (4 g Fibre, 6 g Sugar); 34 g Protein; 1650 mg Sodium

Weiner Schnitzel

This German dish can be made with veal or pork. We've chosen boneless pork chops in our version, pounded thin and coated with seasoned bread crumbs. Traditionally, weiner schnitzel is pan fried in generous amounts of oil, but the air fryer cooks these cutlets perfectly without all the oil. Serve with fries and a garden salad on the side, and sprinkle with fresh herbs for an attractive presentation. If you have any leftovers, they make a fantastic sandwich.

Boneless pork chops (about 6 oz., 170 g, each)	4	4
All-purpose flour	1/2 cup	125 mL
Garlic powder	1 tsp.	5 mL
Salt	1 tsp.	5 mL
Black pepper	1/2 tsp.	2 mL
Large eggs	2	2
Lemon juice	1 tbsp.	15 mL
Panko bread crumbs	2 cups	500 mL
Lemon wedges	4	4

Trim any extra fat off chops. Lay chops on counter in between two layers of plastic food wrap. Pound out each chop to about 1/4 inch (6 mm) thick.

Combine flour and seasonings in a shallow bowl.

Combine eggs and lemon juice in a separate shallow bowl.

Place panko bread crumbs in another shallow bowl. Coat cutlets in flour mixture, shaking off any excess. Dip into egg mixture and then coat in panko bread crumbs. Spray cutlets with vegetable oil spray. Transfer 2 cutlets to air fryer basket. Cook at 375°F (190°C) until breading is golden brown, about 10 minutes, flipping halfway through. Transfer to a plate and cover to keep warm. Repeat with remaining cutlets.

Serve with lemon wedges. Makes 4 servings.

Combo air fryer: Cook for 14 minutes, flipping halfway through.

1 serving: 430 Calories; 17 g Total Fat (7 g Mono, 2 g Poly, 6 g Sat); 200 mg Cholesterol; 29 g Carbohydrate (1 g Fibre, 0 g Sugar); 36 g Protein; 740 mg Sodium

Curried Pork Empanadas

Cream cheese pastry is wrapped around curried ground pork and air fried until golden and crispy! The egg wash really helps brown the pastry.

Cream cheese	2 cups	500 mL
Unsalted butter, softened	1 cup	250 mL
Salt	1/2 tsp.	2 mL
All-purpose flour	3 cups	750 mL
Olive oil	2 tbsp.	30 mL
Ground pork	1 lb.	454 g
Olive oil	2 tbsp.	30 mL
Yellow onion, finely chopped	1/2	1/2
Garlic cloves, minced	2	2
Finely chopped fresh white mushrooms	1 cup	250 mL
Curry powder	1 tsp.	5 mL
Ground cardamom	1 tsp.	5 mL
Allspice	1 tsp.	5 mL
Raisins	1/3 cup	75 mL
Sherry vinegar	2 tbsp.	30 mL
Tamari	1/2 tsp.	2 mL
Brown sugar	2 tsp.	10 mL
Cornstarch	1 tsp.	5 mL
Large egg, fork-beaten	1	1

For the dough, beat first 3 ingredients with a mixer until creamy.

Slowly add flour, stirring by hand until incorporated. Divide dough into 2 small balls. On a floured work surface, roll one ball out with a rolling pin into a 1/2 inch (12 mm) thick circle. Repeat with other dough ball. Cover each with plastic wrap on top, then, flip over onto a tray and cover other side. Refrigerate for at least 1 hour and up to 2 days.

For the filling, heat first amount of olive oil in a large frying pan on medium. Add pork and cook until browned. Transfer to a bowl and set aside.

Heat remaining olive oil in same frying pan on medium. Add onion and cook until softened. Add garlic and mushrooms and cook for 3 minutes. Add curry powder, cardamom, allspice and raisins and mix well.

Add pork and next 4 ingredients and mix well, breaking up any big pieces of pork with your spoon. Cook on low for about 7 minutes, allowing flavours to blend and mixture to thicken slightly.

To make the empanadas, remove dough from fridge and roll out to 1/8 inch (3 mm) thickness. Do not overwork dough. Cut out 6 inch (15 cm) circles. In a small bowl, whisk egg and brush on each circle as you go. Place 1/3 cup (75 mL) pork mixture near centre of each circle. Fold dough over to enclose filling and press edge shut with a fork. Lightly brush with egg. Cook at 325°F (160°C) for 22 minutes. These are best served once cooled. Makes 8 empanadas.

Combo air fryer: Cook for 22 minutes on the lowest rack. Leave in air fryer with heat off for 3 minutes. Set aside to cool before serving.

1 empanada: 420 Calories; 31 g Total Fat (8 g Mono, 1.5 g Poly, 16 g Sat); 95 mg Cholesterol; 23 g Carbohydrate (1 g Fibre, 4 g Sugar); 1 g Protein; 300 mg Sodium

Pork Souvlaki

You can serve these skewers as a main with rice or a Greek salad, or tuck them into pita bread with some chopped lettuce, tomato, thinly sliced red onion and tzatziki. Make sure you soak your bamboo skewers before using them in this recipe or they could burn in the air fryer.

Pork loin, cut into cubes	1 1/2 lbs.	680 g
Salt	1 tsp.	5 mL
Olive oil	3 tbsp.	45 mL
Chopped fresh oregano	2 tbsp.	30 mL
Chopped fresh thyme	1 tbsp.	15 mL
Juice from 1/2 lemon		
Bamboo skewers (8 inches, 20 cm, each), soaked in water for at least 30 minutes	6	6

Season pork cubes with salt and place into a resealable freezer bag. Add olive oil and oregano, thyme and lemon juice. Squeeze air out of bag and seal. Squeeze bag a few times to ensure meat is well coated. Place in fridge for at least 2 hours or overnight. Thread pork onto skewers and cook at 355°F (180°C) for 22 minutes. Makes 6 skewers.

Combo air fryer: Cook for 30 minutes.

1 skewer: 380 Calories; 34 g Total Fat (17 g Mono, 3.5 g Poly, 10 g Sat); 80 mg Cholesterol; 0 g Carbohydrate (0 g Fibre, 0 g Sugar); 18 g Protein; 450 mg Sodium

Herbed Lamb Chops

This is another recipe that works better in the dedicated air fryer. In the combo unit, the lamb did not brown well even though it was cooked through. You may need to cook the lamb in batches, depending on the size of your air fryer.

Lemon juice	1/4 cup	60 mL
Chopped fresh rosemary	2 tbsp.	30 mL
Chopped fresh mint	2 tbsp.	30 mL
Olive oil	2 tbsp.	30 mL
Liquid honey	1 tbsp.	15 mL
Grated lemon zest	1 tbsp.	15 mL
Garlic cloves, minced	3	3
Black pepper	1 tsp.	5 mL
Chili paste	1/2 tsp.	2 mL
Salt	1/2 tsp.	2 mL
Bone-in lamb chops (about 4 oz., 113 g, each)	12	12
Apricot jam	2/3 cup	175 mL
Dijon mustard	1/4 cup	60 mL
Soy sauce	4 tsp.	20 mL
Chopped rosemary	2 tbsp.	30 mL

Combine first 10 ingredients in a large resealable freezer bag.

Place lamb chops in bag. Seal and turn to coat. Marinate in refrigerator for at least 6 hours or overnight, turning bag occasionally. Remove lamb from bag and spray with vegetable oil spray. Cook at 400°F (200°C) for 12 minutes, flipping halfway through. Remove from air fryer and let stand for about 5 minutes.

For the sauce, combine next 3 ingredients in a small saucepan on medium heat. Cook, stirring, for 5 to 7 minutes until jam is melted. Stir in rosemary. Serve with lamb chops. Makes 6 servings.

Combo air fryer: Cook half of lamb chops for 20 minutes, flipping halfway through. Transfer to a plate and cover to keep warm. Repeat with remaining lamb chops.

1 serving: 420 Calories; 23 g Total Fat (10 g Mono, 1 g Poly, 10 g Sat); 95 mg Cholesterol; 26 g Carbohydrate (0 g Fibre, 23 g Sugar); 27 g Protein; 540 mg Sodium

Fried Chicken

This recipe has an exceptionally long marinading time, so plan accordingly. When cooking the chicken, make sure you leave enough space between individual pieces in the air fryer or they will not be crispy.

Bone-in chicken thighs	6	6
(about 5 oz., 140 g, each)		
Chicken drumsticks	6	6
(about 3 oz., 84 g, each)		
Buttermilk (see Tip, page 40)	1 1/2 cups	375 mL
Water	1 1/2 cups	375 mL
Louisiana hot sauce	1 tbsp.	15 mL
Soy sauce	1 tbsp.	15 mL
Worcestershire sauce	1 tsp.	10 mL
Garlic powder	1/2 tsp.	5 mL
All-purpose flour	1 cup	250 mL
Onion powder	1 tsp.	5 mL
Salt	1 tsp.	5 mL
Pepper	1/2 tsp.	2 mL
Baking powder	1/2 tsp.	2 mL
Cayenne powder	1/2 tsp.	2 mL
Poultry seasonings	1/2 tsp.	2 mL
Seasoned salt	1 tsp.	5 mL

Put chicken into a large resealable freezer bag.

Combine next 6 ingredients in a small bowl. Pour over chicken. Seal bag and turn until coated. Let stand in refrigerator for 12 to 14 hours, turning occasionally. Remove chicken. Do not pat dry. Discard any remaining buttermilk mixture.

Combine next 7 ingredients in separate large resealable freezer bag. Add chicken in batches and toss until coated. Discard any remaining flour mixture. Place chicken on a baking sheet and let stand for 10 minutes.

Sprinkle chicken with seasoned salt and spray with vegetable oil spray. Spray air fryer basket with vegetable oil spray. Working in batches so there is enough space in between chicken pieces, cook at 375°F (190°C) until internal temperature reaches 170°F (77°C), about 16 minutes, flipping halfway through. Makes 6 servings.

Combo air fryer: Cook for 20 minutes, flipping halfway through. Remove legs from air fryer and cook thighs for 5 minutes more.

1 serving: 570 Calories; 34 g Total Fat (14 g Mono, 8 g Poly, 10 g Sat); 200 mg Cholesterol; 17 g Carbohydrate (1 g Fibre, 0 g Sugar); 45 g Protein; 920 mg Sodium

Roasted Chicken

A whole chicken may not fit in your air fryer, depending on the size of your machine. If the chicken doesn't fit, you could split it in half and adjust the cooking time accordingly.

Whole chicken (about 3 lbs., 1.4 kg)	1	1
Olive oil	3 tbsp.	45 mL
Chopped fresh rosemary	2 tbsp.	30 mL
Chopped fresh thyme	1 tbsp.	15 mL
Garlic powder	2 tsp.	10 mL
Onion powder	1 tsp.	5 mL
Paprika	1/2 tsp.	2 mL
Salt	1/2 tsp.	2 mL
Black pepper	1/2 tsp.	2 mL

Tie chicken legs together, or to tail, with butcher twine so they do not touch top element of air fryer.

Combine next 8 ingredients in a small bowl. Brush chicken with olive oil mixture, ensuring bottom is coated as well. Place chicken in greased air fryer basket breast side down. Cook at 350°F (175°C) for 25 minutes. Using tongs, carefully turn chicken over to be breast side up. Cook for 20 minutes, until internal temperature reaches 170°F (77°C). Let stand on a board for about 10 minutes before carving. Drizzle with juices, if there are any, from bottom of air fryer basket after carving. Makes 4 servings.

Combo air fryer: Cook for 50 to 55 minutes, placing a piece of parchment paper on the rack so there are no flare ups when the chicken drips.

1 serving: 660 Calories; 22 g Total Fat (12 g Mono, 3.5 g Poly, 4.5 g Sat); 290 mg Cholesterol; 2 g Carbohydrate (0 g Fibre, 0 g Sugar); 106 g Protein; 550 mg Sodium

Popcorn Chicken

For super crispy results, make sure your chicken pieces are in a single layer and well spaced out in the air fryer basket. Spraying the flour-coated chicken with vegetable oil spray before cooking helps the coating get a nice and brown.

Buttermilk (see Tip, page 40)	2 cups	500 mL
Dill pickle brine	1/2 cup	125 mL
Paprika	1 tsp.	5 mL
Salt	1 tsp.	5 mL
Black pepper	1/2 tsp.	2 mL
Boneless, skinless chicken breast, cut into 1 inch (2.5 cm) pieces	2 lbs.	900 g
All-purpose flour	2 cups	500 mL
Garlic powder	2 tsp.	10 mL
Onion powder	2 tsp.	10 mL
Paprika	2 tsp.	10 mL
Salt	2 tsp.	10 mL
Black pepper	1 tsp.	5 mL

Combine first 5 ingredients in a large resealable bag. Add chicken and marinate in the refrigerator for at least 2 and up to 4 hours.

Combine next 6 ingredients in a shallow bowl. Remove chicken from marinade and transfer marinade to a separate shallow bowl. Working in batches, cover chicken pieces in flour mixture, shaking off excess. Dip into buttermilk mixture and then again into flour mixture, shaking off excess flour. Set coated chicken pieces aside and repeat with remaining chicken pieces until all chicken is coated. Spray chicken pieces with vegetable oil spray and carefully transfer to air fryer basket. Cook at 375°F (190°C) until golden, about 14 minutes, shaking basket halfway through. Makes 6 servings.

Combo air fryer: Cook for 22 minutes, shaking and rotating the basket halfway through.

1 serving: 340 Calories; 3 g Total Fat (1 g Mono, 1 g Poly, .5 g Sat); 90 mg Cholesterol; 34 g Carbohydrate (1 g Fibre, 0 g Sugar); 39 g Protein; 690 mg Sodium

Butter Chicken Pockets

Why eat your butter chicken with rice when you can have it in a crispy, golden hand-held pocket instead? The current popularity of butter chicken pizza was the inspiration for this recipe, but we discovered that butter puff pastry works even better than pizza dough!

Boneless, skinless chicken breast halves (about 4 oz., 113 g, each), cut into 1 inch (2.5 cm) pieces	3	3
Salt	1 tsp.	5 mL
Black pepper	1 tsp.	5 mL
Olive oil	2 tbsp.	30 mL
Olive oil	1 tbsp.	15 mL
Large red onion, thinly sliced	1	1
Garlic paste	1 tbsp.	15 mL
Ginger paste	1 tbsp.	15 mL
Butter chicken sauce	1 1/2 cups	375 mL
Half and half cream	1 cup	250mL
Ketchup	1 tbsp.	15 mL
Butter	2 tbsp.	30 mL
Chopped fresh cilantro	3 tbsp.	45 mL
Packages of butter puff pastry (14 oz., 397 mL)	2	2
Grated mozzarella cheese	1 1/2 cups	375mL
Chopped fresh cilantro	2 tbsp.	30 mL

Season chicken with salt and pepper. Heat first amount of oil in a medium frying pan on medium-high. Add chicken and cook until browned, about 10 minutes. Transfer to a bowl and set aside.

Heat remaining oil in same pan on medium-high. Add onion and cook until golden brown, about 7 minutes. Add garlic and ginger pastes and cook for 1 minute. Stir in chicken.

Stir in next 4 ingredients and cook, covered, for 1 hour. Stir in cilantro and simmer, uncovered, for 30 minutes until thickened.

Lay out puff pastry and cut into 6 inch (15 cm) circles. Add 1/3 cup (75 mL) butter chicken mixture to one side of each circle and sprinkle with an even amount mozzarella and chopped cilantro. Fold dough over to enclose filling and pinch edges together. Spray both sides of each pocket with vegetable oil spray. Cook at 390°F (198°C) for 7 minutes, flipping halfway through. Makes 8 pockets.

Combo air fryer: Cook for 20 minutes, flipping halfway through.

1 pocket: 510 Calories; 33 g Total Fat (4.5 g Mono, 1 g Poly, 15 g Sat); 80 mg Cholesterol; 33 g Carbohydrate (1 g Fibre, 5 g Sugar); 18 g Protein; 840 mg Sodium

Piri Piri Chicken

This chicken dish, with roots in both Portugal and Africa, has exploded in popularity over the past few years. So, of course we had to try it in the air fryer!

Dried crushed chilies	1/2 tbsp.	7 mL
Grated garlic	1 tbsp.	15 mL
Lime juice	2 tbsp.	30 mL
Smoked paprika	1 tbsp.	15 mL
Chopped fresh oregano	1 tbsp.	15 mL
Salt	1/2 tsp.	2 mL
Black pepper	1/4 tsp.	1 mL
Boneless, skinless chicken thighs (about 4 oz., 113 g, each)	8	8

Combine first 8 ingredients in a large bowl. Add chicken and stir to coat. Marinate, covered, in refrigerator for 1 hour. Cook at 350°F (175°C) for 18 minutes, flipping halfway through.

Combo air fryer: Cook for 30 minutes, flipping halfway through. Makes 4 servings.

1 serving: 350 Calories; 15 g Total Fat (7 g Mono, 3 g Poly, 3.5 g Sat); 210 mg Cholesterol; 1 g Carbohydrate (0 g Fibre, 0 g Sugar); 50 g Protein; 370 mg Sodium

Stuffed Prosciutto-wrapped Chicken Breasts

Tender chicken stuffed with cheese and wrapped with salty prosciutto. The air fryer seems to concentrate salty flavours, so be sure to use thinly sliced prosciutto so the salt doesn't overwhelm the other flavours in this dish.

Chopped sundried tomatoes in oil, drained	1/4 cup	60 mL
Ricotta cheese	1/4 cup	60 mL
Chopped fresh rosemary	1 tbsp.	15 mL
Chopped fresh thyme	1 tsp.	5 mL
Boneless, skinless chicken breasts (about 6 oz., 170 g, each)	4	4
Prosciutto slices	8	8

Combine first 4 ingredients in a small bowl.

Lay chicken breasts flat on a cutting board. Using a sharp knife, slice into one side of each chicken breast, being careful not to cut all the way through to other side, making a pocket.

Spoon about 2 tbsp. (30 mL) ricotta mixture into each pocket. Wrap 2 slices of prosciutto tightly around each chicken breast. Spray with vegetable oil. Transfer chicken to an air fryer basket and cook at 375°F (190°C) for 14 minutes, flipping halfway through. Chicken is cooked when internal temperature reaches 165°F (74°C). Let stand for 5 minutes before serving. Makes 4 servings.

Combo air fryer: Cook for 20 to 22 minutes, flipping halfway through.

1 serving: 300 Calories; 10 g Total Fat (2 g Mono, 1 g Poly, 4 g Sat); 130 mg Cholesterol; 2 g Carbohydrate (0 g Fibre, 0 g Sugar); 49 g Protein; 680 mg Sodium

Persian Chicken Skewers

These delicious skewers need to marinate overnight, so plan accordingly. The saffron lemon butter sauce takes these skewers to the next level, but they are also delicious without it. Serve with basmati rice, roasted halved tomatoes and fresh onion.

Saffron, ground	1 tsp.	5 mL
Warm water	2 tbsp.	30 mL
White onion, thinly sliced	2	2
Plain yogurt	1/2 cup	125 mL
Olive oil	3 tbsp.	45 mL
Garlic cloves, diced	2	2
Salt	1 1/2 tsp.	7 mL
Boneless, skinless chicken breast, (4 oz., 113 g, each) cut into 1 inch (2.5 cm) cubes	3	3
Saffron	1/2 tsp.	2 mL
Warm water	2 tbsp.	30 mL
Unsalted butter	1/4 cup	60 mL
Lemon juice	1/4 cup	60 mL

Combine saffron and water in a small cup, stirring until saffron is dissolved.

Combine next 5 ingredients in a large bowl. Stir in saffron mixture. Add chicken and stir to coat. Marinate, covered, in refrigerator overnight. Thread chicken onto metal skewers, discarding any remaining marinade. Cook at 350°F (175°C) for 22 minutes, flipping halfway through.

For the sauce, combine second amount of saffron and water in a small cup, stirring until saffron is dissolved.

Melt butter in a small saucepan over medium. Stir in saffron mixture and lemon juice. Drizzle over chicken. Makes 4 skewers.

Combo air fryer: Cook for 30 minutes, flipping halfway through.

1 skewer with 2 tbsp. (30 mL) sauce: 250 Calories; 16 g Total Fat (6 g Mono, 1 g Poly, 8 g Sat); 80 mg Cholesterol; 6 g Carbohydrate (0 g Fibre, 2 g Sugar); 21 g Protein; 360 mg Sodium

Parmesan Turkey Cutlets

Thanks to the size of the turkey breasts, you will most likely have to cook these cutlets in batches. For best results, be sure to shake off any extra flour during the breading stage. Too much flour will prevent your coating from getting nice and crispy.

Turkey cutlets (about 6 oz., 170 g, each)	4	4
Salt	1 tsp.	5 mL
Black pepper	1/2 tsp.	2 mL
All-purpose flour	1 cup	250 mL
Garlic powder	1 tsp.	5 mL
Salt	1 tsp.	5 mL
Dried parsley	1/2 tsp.	2 mL
Black pepper	1/2 tsp.	2 mL
Large egg	2	2
Buttermilk (see Tip, page 40)	1/4 cup	60 mL
Dry bread crumbs (see Tip, page 134)	2 cups	500 mL
Grated Parmesan cheese	1/2 cup	125 mL
Chopped fresh parsley	2 tbsp.	30 mL

Season cutlets with salt and pepper.

Combine next 5 ingredients in a shallow bowl.

Beat egg and buttermilk together in a separate shallow bowl.

Combine panko and Parmesan in another shallow bowl. Coat cutlets in flour mixture, shaking off any excess. Dip into egg mixture and then into panko mixture, turning until evenly coated. Spray cutlets with vegetable oil spray and transfer to air fryer tray. Cook at 375°F (190°C) until breading is golden brown, about 10 minutes, flipping cutlets over halfway through. If cooking in batches, transfer cooked cutlets to a plate and cover to keep warm. Repeat with remaining cutlets. Sprinkle with parsley. Makes 4 servings.

Combo air fryer: Cook for 14 minutes, flipping halfway through.

1 serving: 490 Calories; 8 g Total Fat (2 g Mono, 1 g Poly, 3 g Sat); 200 mg Cholesterol; 54 g Carbohydrate (2 g Fibre, 2 g Sugar); 50 g Protein; 1330 mg Sodium

Lemon Herb Turkey Breast

Not everything you cook in your air fryer needs to be breaded. Sometimes you just want a nice, light-tasting dinner, and this turkey breast sure delivers! Serve with Sage and Onion Stuffing Balls (page 144) and Bacon and Pomegranate Brussel's Sprouts (page 146).

Olive oil	1/4 cup	60 mL
Lemon juice	3 tbsp.	45 mL
Garlic cloves, minced	4	4
Chopped fresh rosemary	3 tbsp.	45 mL
Chopped fresh thyme	2 tbsp.	30 mL
Chopped fresh sage	1 tbsp.	15 mL
Dijon mustard	1 tbsp.	15 mL
Salt	1 tsp.	5 mL
Black pepper	1/2 tsp.	2 mL
Paprika	1/4 tsp.	1 mL
Bone in, skin-on turkey breast (about 2 1/2 lbs., 1.1 kg)	1	1

Combine first 10 ingredients in a small bowl.

Carefully loosen skin, but do not remove. Stuff 3 tbsp. (45 mL) of lemon herb mixture between meat and skin, spreading mixture as evenly as possible. Brush remaining mixture onto turkey breast. Spray air fryer basket with vegetable oil spray. Place turkey breast skin side down in basket and cook at 350°F (175°C) for 25 minutes. Using tongs, flip turkey breast over so skin side is up, and cook until internal temperature reaches 170°F (77°C), about 20 minutes. Let stand for 10 minutes before carving. Drizzle with juices, if there are any, from bottom of air fryer basket after carving. Makes 4 servings.

Combo air fryer: Cook for 50 minutes, flipping halfway through.

1 serving: 490 Calories; 30 g Total Fat (16 g Mono, 5 g Poly, 6 g Sat); 150 mg Cholesterol; 3 g Carbohydrate (0 g Fibre, 0 g Sugar); 50 g Protein; 770 mg Sodium

Saskatoon Duck Breast

Rich duck smothered with a homemade saskaton berry sauce—this elegant dish is sure to wow everyone you serve it to.

Duck breast, fat trimmed (6 oz., 170 g, each)	4	4
Saskatoon berries, fresh or frozen	2 cups	500 mL
Chicken broth	1 cup	250 mL
Garlic cloves, minced	2	2
Green peppercorns	1 tbsp.	15 mL
Chopped fresh rosemary	1 tbsp.	15 mL
Chopped fresh thyme	1 tbsp.	15 mL
Salt	1 tsp.	5 mL
Sugar	1/3 cup	75 mL
Lemon juice	2 tbsp.	30 mL
Cornstarch	2 tsp.	10 mL

Score skin of each breast in a diagonal pattern, without cutting down to meat.

Combine next 6 ingredients in a large resealable plastic bag. Add duck and marinate in refrigerator for up to 2 hours. Remove duck from marinade and set marinade aside. Sprinkle duck with salt. Grease air fryer basket and add duck, skin side up. Cook at 400°F (200°C) for 10 minutes, without disturbing.

For the sauce, put reserved marinade in a small saucepan. Bring to a boil and simmer for about 7 to 8 minutes, until reduced by about a quarter. Carefully mash about half saskatoons in sauce. Whisk in sugar. Combine lemon juice and cornstarch in a small cup and gradually whisk into sauce. Boil until thickened, whisking constantly, about 5 minutes. Brush about 1 tbsp. (15 mL) sauce on each duck breast and cook for 2 minutes. Remove from air fryer and let stand for 5 minutes. Serve with remaining sauce. Makes 4 servings.

Combo air fryer: Cook for 14 minutes without disturbing. Brush with sauce and cook for 4 minutes.

1 serving: 710 Calories; 56 g Total Fat (27 g Mono, 7 g Poly, 19 g Sat); 110 mg Cholesterol; 32 g Carbohydrate (4 g Fibre, 17 g Sugar); 17 g Protein; 850 mg Sodium

Air-fried Chicken Sandwiches

For this dish, your chicken breasts should be an even thickness, but you do not want to pound them into a thin cutlet. Spraying the chicken with peanut oil gives it that great deep-fried flavour without the need for deep-frying. Serve with Chipotle Aioli (page 162) or whip up a batch of spicy mayonnaise (see sidebar, page 105).

Buttermilk	1 cup	250 mL
Dill pickle brine	1/2 cup	125 mL
Hot sauce	1 tbsp.	15 mL
Boneless, skinless chicken breasts (about 6 oz., 170 g, each)	4	4
All-purpose flour	1 cup	250 mL
Cornstarch	3 tbsp.	45 mL
Icing (confectioner's) sugar	2 tbsp.	30 mL
Garlic powder	1 tsp.	5 mL
Onion powder	1 tsp.	5 mL
Paprika	1 tsp.	5 mL
Salt	1 tsp.	5 mL
Dried dill	1/2 tsp.	2 mL
Dried thyme	1/2 tsp.	2 mL
Ground sage	1/2 tsp.	2 mL
Black pepper	1/4 tsp.	1 mL
Large eggs, fork beaten	2	2
Brioche buns, toasted	4	4
Spicy mayonnaise (see sidebar, page 105)	1/2 cup	125 mL
Tomato slices	8	8
Coleslaw	1 cup	250 mL
Sliced dill pickles	2	2

Combine first 3 ingredients in a large resealable freezer bag.

Place chicken breasts between 2 sheets of parchment paper and pound lightly until all breasts are an even thickness (do not flatten!) Add chicken to freezer bag and marinate in refrigerator for 30 minutes up to 2 hours.

Combine next 11 ingredients in a shallow bowl. Place eggs in a separate shallow bowl.

Remove chicken from marinade and whisk marinade into eggs. Coat chicken in flour mixture, shaking off any excess. Dip into egg mixture, allowing excess to drip off, and then again into flour mixture. Spray chicken with peanut oil and cook at 400°F (200°C) until chicken reaches 165°F (74°C) internally, about 12 minutes, flipping halfway through. Set aside to cool slightly.

Spread buns with mayonnaise. Top with chicken breast, remaining 3 ingredients and upper half of bun. Makes 4 sandwiches.

Combo air fryer: Cook for 16 to 18 minutes, flipping halfway through.

1 sandwich: 850 Calories; 33 g Total Fat (14 g Mono, 7 g Poly, 33 g Sat); 240 mg Cholesterol; 75 g Carbohydrate (3 g Fibre, 11 g Sugar); 54 g Protein; 1600 mg Sodium

To make spicy mayonnaise, add 2 minced garlic cloves, 1 tbsp. (15 mL) hot pepper sauce and 1 tsp. (5 mL) smoked paprika to 1/2 cup (125 mL) mayonnaise and stir well.

Coconut Prawns with Paprika Aioli

If you are using frozen prawns, take them out of the freezer a few hours before you plan to use them, or even the night before, and let them thaw in the fridge.

Mayonnaise	3 tbsp.	45 mL
Lime juice, fresh	1 tsp.	5 mL
Paprika	1 tsp.	5 mL
Salt	1/4 tsp.	1 mL
Paprika	1/4 tsp.	1 mL
Black pepper	1/4 tsp.	1 mL
Hot sauce	1 tsp.	5 mL
Large egg, fork-beaten	2	2
Uncooked large prawns, peeled, tails intact	24	24
Panko bread crumbs	3/4 cup	175 mL
Sweetened coconut flakes	1/2 cup	125 mL
Chopped fresh cilantro	1 tbsp.	15 mL
Paprika	1 tsp.	5 mL
Salt	1 tsp.	5 mL
Black pepper	1/4 tsp.	1 mL
Chopped fresh cilantro, for garnish	1 tbsp.	15 mL

For the aioli, combine first 7 ingredients in a small bowl and refrigerate until ready to serve.

For the prawns, whisk egg in a large bowl. Add prawns and set in refrigerator to marinade for about 10 minutes.

In a small bowl, combine next 6 ingredients and mix well. Coat each prawn in coconut mixture and spray lightly with vegetable oil spray. Cook at 325°F (160°C) for 10 minutes, flipping halfway through. Garnish with remaining cilantro. Makes 4 servings.

Combo air fryer: Cook for 12 minutes, flipping and spraying again with vegetable oil spray halfway through.

1 serving: 290 Calories; 15 g Total Fat (6 g Mono, 3.5 g Poly, 4.5 g Sat); 240 mg Cholesterol; 14 g Carbohydrate (1 g Fibre, 4 g Sugar); 22 g Protein; 1040 mg Sodium

Bacon-wrapped Scallops

Depending on the size of your air fryer, you may need to cook these scallops in batches to ensure they are in a single layer and well spaced out. Otherwise the bacon will not crisp up nicely. Serve with a buttered or light cream-based pasta dish on the side.

Double smoked bacon slices	12	12
Fresh scallops	12	12
Chopped fresh chives	2 tbsp.	30 mL
Salt, to taste		
Black pepper, to taste		
Chopped fresh thyme, for garnish	2 tbsp.	30 mL

Place bacon in air fryer, leaving room in between each piece, and cook at 325°F (160°C) for 12 minutes. Transfer to a plate lined with paper towel to drain and cool slightly.

Wrap each scallop with a piece of bacon, trimming bacon if necessary so it wraps nicely around scallop. Secure with a toothpick. Season with first amount of chives and salt and pepper, if desired. Cook at 325°F (160°C) for 15 minutes, in batches if necessary, to ensure scallops are in a single layer and well spaced out.

Garnish with fresh thyme. Serve immediately. Makes 4 servings.

Combo air fryer: Cook bacon for 12 minutes. Cook bacon-wrapped scallops for 15 minutes.

1 serving: 590 Calories; 53 g Total Fat (23 g Mono, 6 g Poly, 17 g Sat); 100 mg Cholesterol; 2 g Carbohydrate (0 g Fibre, 0 g Sugar); 24 g Protein; 1050 mg Sodium

Crab-stuffed Portobellos

Although you might generally think of stuffed mushrooms as an appetizer, these beauties–stuffed with crab and Gruyere cheese—are hearty enough for a nice light supper. Serve with a fresh garden salad on the side.

Large portobello mushrooms	4	4
Olive oil	3 tbsp.	45 mL
Large yellow onion, diced	1/2	1/2
Garlic cloves, minced	3	3
Can of crabmeat, drained (4.25 oz., 120 g)	1	1
Dried thyme	1 tsp.	5 mL
Salt	1/2 tsp.	2 mL
Black pepper	1/2 tsp.	2 mL
Dried oregano	1/2 tsp.	2 mL
Cream cheese	4 oz.	113 g
Chopped fresh chives	3 tbsp.	45 mL
Grated Gruyere cheese	3/4 cup	175 mL

Remove stems from mushrooms, chop and set aside. Using a spoon, remove gills from mushroom caps and discard. Set aside.

Heat oil in a medium saucepan on medium-high. Add onion and cook until softened, about 7 minutes. Turn heat to medium-low and add garlic and reserved mushroom stems. Cook, stirring occasionally, for 5 minutes. Set aside to cool completely.

Add crab, thyme, salt, pepper, oregano, cream cheese and chives, stirring well. Spray bottoms of mushrooms with vegetable oil spray. Fill mushroom caps with mixture and sprinkle with grated gruyere. Cook at 325°F (160°C) for 10 minutes. Makes 4 stuffed mushrooms.

Combo air fryer: Cook for 10 minutes.

1 mushroom: 340 Calories; 26 g Total Fat (9 g Mono, 1.5 g Poly, 11 g Sat); 75 mg Cholesterol; 10 g Carbohydrate (2 g Fibre, 4 g Sugar); 16 g Protein; 530 mg Sodium

Air-fried Halibut Filets

If you've got a hankering for fish and chips, pair these tasty filets with Double Air-fried Fries (page 150) and serve with tartar sauce, coleslaw and thick wedges of fresh lemon!

All-purpose flour	3/4 cup	175 mL
Cornstarch	7 tbsp.	105 mL
Baking soda	1 tsp.	5 mL
Soda water	2/3 cup	175 mL
Large egg	1	1
All-purpose flour	1/2 cup	125 mL
Sea salt	1 tsp.	5 mL
Black pepper	1/2 tsp.	2 mL
Paprika	1/2 tsp.	2 mL
Cayenne pepper, to taste		
Halibut filets	4	4

Combine first amount of flour, cornstarch and baking soda in a large bowl. Add soda water and egg, stirring until smooth. Cover with plastic wrap and let stand in refrigerator for 20 minutes.

In another bowl, mix remaining flour, salt, pepper, paprika and cayenne.

Pat fish down with paper towel to dry. Coat fish in flour mixturen, shaking off any excess, and then in batter. Cook at 350°F (175°C) for 20 minutes, flipping halfway through. Makes 4 filets.

Combo air fryer: Cook for 20 minutes, flipping halfway through.

1 filet: 380 Calories; 6 g Total Fat (2 g Mono, 2 g Poly, 1 g Sat); 100 mg Cholesterol; 43 g Carbohydrate (1 g Fibre, 0 g Sugar); 35 g Protein; 1000 mg Sodium

Cod Taquitos with Mango Avocado Salsa

These crispy taquitos are stuffed with cod, feta and a fresh homemade mango avocado salsa. The salsa will keep in the fridge in an airtight container for about 3 days.

Mangoes, peeled, and finely chopped	1	1
Medium beefsteak tomato, chopped, seeds discarded	1/2	1/2
Medium red onion, diced	1/4 cup	60 mL
Medium yellow pepper, diced	1/2	1/2
Chopped fresh parsley	1 tbsp.	15 mL
Brown sugar	1 tbsp.	15 mL
Lime juice	2 tsp.	10 mL
Zest from 1 lime		
Apple cider vinegar	1/2 tsp.	2 mL
Hot sauce, to taste		
Medium avocado, diced	1/2	1/2
Skinless cod, thawed if frozen cut into 1 inch (2.5 cm) thick pieces	1 lb.	454 g
Paprika	1 tbsp.	15 mL
Salt	1 tsp.	5 mL
Black pepper	1 tsp.	5 mL
Zest from 1 lime		
Feta	3/4 cup	175 mL
Flour tortilla shells (6 inch, 15 cm, diameter)	12	12
Chopped fresh cilantro	1 tsp.	5 mL
Sour cream	1/2 cup	125 mL
Lime wedges	12	12

For the salsa, combine first 11 ingredients in a large bowl. Let stand in refrigerator for about an hour.

Toss cod with paprika, salt, pepper and lime zest ensuring it is well coated. Spray with vegetable oil spray. Cook at 350°F (175°C) for 5 minutes, flipping halfway through. Let stand for 4 minutes. Flake fish with a fork.

salsa and sprinkle with cilantro. Roll tortillas as tightly as possible, securing with a toothpick. Spray with vegetable oil spray. Cook at 350°F (175°C) for 7 minutes, flipping halfway through.

Serve with remaining salsa, sour cream and lime wedges.

Combo air fryer: Cook cod for 6 minutes, flipping halfway through. Cook taquitos for 5 to 6 minutes, flipping halfway through. Makes 12 taquitos.

1 taquito: 210 Calories; 7 g Total Fat (2 g Mono, 0.5 g Poly, 2.5 g Sat); 25 mg Cholesterol; 26 g Carbohydrate (3 g Fibre, 9 g Sugar); 11 g Protein; 510 mg Sodium

Maple Soy Glazed Salmon

This salmon is the perfect combination of salty and sweet, with just a little heat from the sriracha. Serve with a side of brown or basmati rice and some steamed veggies.

Soy sauce	2 tbsp.	30 mL
Mirin	1 tsp.	5 mL
Maple syrup	3 tbsp.	45 mL
Sriracha	1 tbsp.	15 mL
Minced garlic	1 tsp.	5 mL
Ginger root, peeled, minced	1 tbsp.	15 mL
Salmon filets (about 5 oz., 140 g, each)	4	4
Chopped fresh cilantro, optional	1 tbsp.	15 mL
Black or white sesame seeds	1 tbsp.	15 mL

Combine first 6 ingredients in a resealable freezer bag.

Add salmon and marinate in refrigerator for 30 minutes. Remove fish from marinade and transfer to air fryer tray. Pour marinade into a medium saucepan and set aside. Cook salmon at 350°F (175°C) for 12 minutes, flipping halfway through.

Heat marinade on medium until it thickens slightly. Drizzle over salmon and garnish with cilantro and sesame seeds. Makes 4 servings.

Combo air fryer: Cook for 12 minutes, flipping halfway through.

1 serving: 250 Calories; 10 g Total Fat (3.5 g Mono, 4 g Poly, 1.5 g Sat); 80 mg Cholesterol; 9 g Carbohydrate (0 g Fibre, 8 g Sugar); 30 g Protein; 610 mg Sodium

Crispy Cod Sticks

Who doesn't love fish sticks! No need to buy the premade frozen version from the supermarket freezer section when you can make an even tastier version at home in your air fryer. Serve with fresh lemon or lime wedges. The coconut burns easily in the combo air fryer, so you might consider leaving it out of the breading and just sprinkle it on at the end.

Large egg, fork-beaten	2	2
Salt	1 tsp.	5 mL
Black pepper	1 tsp.	5 mL
Half and half cream	1/4 cup	60 mL
Skinless cod, thawed if frozen, cut into 1 inch (2.5 cm) thick pieces	1 lb.	454 g
Garlic powder	1/4 tsp.	1 mL
Italian seasoning	1/4 tsp.	1 mL
Panko bread crumbs	1/2 cup	125mL
Chopped fresh parsley	2 tbsp.	30 mL
Sweetened coconut flakes	1/4 cup	60 mL

Combine egg, salt, pepper and cream in a shallow bowl. Add cod and marinate, covered, in refrigerator for 30 minutes.

In a separate bowl, combine garlic powder, Italian seasoning, panko, first amount of parsley and coconut. Dip each fish stick in panko herb mixture to coat all sides, gently shaking off any excess. Spray with vegetable oil spray. Cook at 325°F (160°C) for 12 minutes, flipping halfway through. Makes 4 servings.

Combo air fryer: Cook on the lowest rack for 12 minutes, flipping halfway through.

1 serving: 200 Calories; 6 g Total Fat (1 g Mono, 0.5 g Poly, 3.5 g Sat); 160 mg Cholesterol; 9 g Carbohydrate (0 g Fibre, 3 g Sugar); 25 g Protein; 720 mg Sodium

Stuffed Eggplants

Stuffed eggplants are a simple, versatile and delicious vegetarian meal. In this dish, we've given the eggplant Greek flavours and stuffed them with a mixture of quinoa, tomato, peppers and olives.

Eggplants (about 1 lb., 454 g, each)	2	2
Lemon juice	1 tbsp.	15 mL
Olive oil	1 tbsp.	15 mL
Chopped medium red onion	1	1
Chopped medium red pepper	1	1
Ground cumin	1 tbsp.	15 mL
Garlic cloves, minced	2	2
Chopped fresh oregano	2 tsp.	10 mL
Medium tomatoes, seeded and diced	2	2
Cooked quinoa	1 cup	250 mL
Tomato paste	1 tbsp.	15 mL
Salt	1 1/2 tsp.	7 mL
Chopped, pitted Kalamata olives	1/2 cup	125 mL
Chopped Italian parsley	1/2 cup	125 mL
Red wine vinegar	1 tbsp.	15 mL
Crumbled feta cheese	1/4 cup	60 mL
Chopped fresh oregano	2 tsp.	10 mL

Cut eggplants in half lengthwise. Carefully scoop out flesh leaving a 1/2 inch (12 mm) border on bottom and sides. Transfer flesh to a cutting board and chop. Place in a small bowl and toss with lemon juice. Set aside. Spray eggplants with vegetable oil spray.

Heat olive oil in a large frying pan on medium. Add onion and red pepper. Cook for 6 to 8 minutes, stirring occasionally, until onion and red pepper are soft. Stir in next 3 ingredients and cook until fragrant, about 2 minutes.

Stir in next 4 ingredients and reserved eggplant flesh. Cook, covered, for about 8 to 10 minutes, stirring occasionally, until vegetables are soft. Remove from heat and stir in olives, parsley and red wine vinegar. Transfer eggplant shells to air fryer tray and cook at 375°F (190°C) for 5 minutes.

Remove shells from air fryer and divide filling evenly among eggplants. Working in batches if necessary, cook stuffed eggplants for 10 minutes each. Remove from air fryer, sprinkle with feta cheese, and cook for 2 minutes.

Remove from air fryer and sprinkle with oregano. Makes 4 servings.

Combo air fryer: Cook eggplant shells for 7 minutes undisturbed. Stuff with filling and cook for 16 minutes, rotating basket halfway through. Sprinkle with feta cheese and cook for 2 minutes.

1 serving: 280 Calories; 12 g Total Fat (6 g Mono, 1.5 g Poly, 2 g Sat); 10 mg Cholesterol; 40 g Carbohydrate (14 g Fibre, 12 g Sugar); 9 g Protein; 1370 mg Sodium

Cajun Cauliflower Steaks

These delicious cauliflower steaks are a great vegetarian entree! Perfect for meatless Mondays, or any day of the week! Serve with mashed or roasted potatoes and steamed veggies, or a rice or quinoa pilaf.

Paprika	2 tbsp.	30 mL
Garlic powder	1 tbsp.	15 mL
Onion powder	2 tsp.	10 mL
Black pepper	2 tsp.	10 mL
Dried thyme	2 tsp.	10 mL
Dried oregano	2 tsp.	10 mL
Salt	2 tsp.	10 mL
Mustard powder	1 tsp.	5 mL
Dried crushed chilies	1/2 tsp.	2 mL
Medium head of cauliflower	1	1
Chopped parsley	2 tbsp.	30 mL
Lime wedges	4	4

Combine first 9 ingredients in a small bowl and set aside.

Wash and clean cauliflower. Trim leaves and bottom stem, leaving core intact. Carefully slice through middle, ensuring florets are intact. Cut four 1 inch (2.5 cm) steaks from middle of cauliflower. Spray cauliflower with vegetable oil spray. Rub spice mixture mix onto both sides of steaks, ensuring they are well covered. Transfer steaks to air fryer basket and cook at 350°F (175°C) for 16 minutes, flipping halfway through.

Remove from air fryer and let stand for 5 minutes before serving. Sprinkle with parsley and serve with lime wedges. Makes 4 steaks.

Combo air fryer: Cook for 25 minutes, flipping halfway through.

1 steak: 70 Calories; 1 g Total Fat (0 g Mono, 0 g Poly, 0 g Sat); 0 mg Cholesterol; 13 g Carbohydrate (4 g Fibre, 4 g Sugar); 4 g Protein; 1210 mg Sodium

Veggie Pizza with Broccoli Parmesan Crust

Once you have tasted pizza from the air fryer, you will never go back to pizza from the oven again! We've replaced the traditional wheat crust with a delicious broccoli-based crust with fantastic results. The dough for the crust may seem to be too wet at first, but it will dry out as you work it.

Fresh asparagus spears, trimmed of tough ends	12	12
Olive oil	1 tsp.	5 mL
Paprika	1/2 tsp.	2 mL
Large head of broccoli	1	1
Grated Parmesan cheese	1/2 cup	125 mL
Large eggs, fork-beaten	3	3
Grated old Cheddar cheese	1 cup	250 mL
Dried oregano	1 tbsp.	15 mL
Salt	1/4 tsp.	1 mL
Dried thyme	1 tsp.	5 mL
Onion powder	1/4 tsp.	1 mL
Garlic powder	1/4 tsp.	1 mL
Chopped fresh basil	1 tsp.	5 mL
Pizza sauce	1/4 cup	60 mL
Red onion, thinly sliced	1/2 cup	125 mL
Grated white Cheddar cheese	1/2 cup	125 mL
Chopped fresh basil	1/4 cup	60 mL

Combine asparagus, olive oil and paprika in a large bowl. Cook at 375°F (190°C) for 8 minutes. Let stand until cool enough to handle. Chop and set aside.

For the crust, cut broccoli into small chunks and place in a food processor. Pulse until broccoli resembles rice. Transfer 2 cups (500 mL) to a medium non-stick frying pan (reserve remaining broccoli for another purpose) and cook on medium heat for 2 to 3 minutes, stirring occasionally. Do not allow broccoli to brown. Remove from heat and set aside to cool. Place cooled broccoli in a clean dish towel and squeeze out as much liquid as possible.

Combine broccoli and next 9 ingredients. Turn dough out onto a piece of parchment paper, shape into a ball and work it with your fist from the inside of the circle outwards to form two 6 inch (15 cm) crusts. Cook at 400°F (200°C) for 14 minutes, flipping halfway through.

Spread each crust with pizza sauce and sprinkle with asparagus, onion and white Cheddar. Cook for 4 minutes. Sprinkle with basil and serve. Makes two 6 inch (15 cm) pizzas.

Combo air fryer: Cook crust for 14 minutes, flipping halfway through. Add toppings and cook for 4 minutes.

1 pizza: 750 Calories; 47 g Total Fat (15 g Mono, 2.5 g Poly, 25 g Sat); 430 mg Cholesterol; 35 g Carbohydrate (12 g Fibre, 11 g Sugar); 53 g Protein; 1590 mg Sodium

Salsa Bean Burgers

The crushed tortilla chips give these burgers a delicious crunch! If you like a little more heat, use hot salsa instead of medium.

Can of red kidney beans (19. oz, 540 g), rinsed and drained	1	1
Large egg, fork-beaten	1	1
Crushed tortilla chips	1 cup	250 mL
Medium salsa	1/2 cup	125 mL
Hamburger buns	5	5

Mash beans with a fork in medium bowl.

Stir in next 3 ingredients. Divide mixture into 5 equal portions. Shape into 4 inch (10 cm) patties. Spray with vegetable oil and transfer to air fryer basket. Cook at 375°F (190°C) until heated through, about 5 minutes, flipping halfway through.

Remove from air fryer and let stand for 4 minutes. Place in buns and top with your favourite toppings. Makes 5 burgers.

Combo air fryer: Cook for 8 minutes, flipping halfway through.

1 burger: 270 Calories; 5 g Total Fat (1 g Mono, 2 g Poly, 1 g Sat); 40 mg Cholesterol; 45 g Carbohydrate (9 g Fibre, 7 g Sugar); 12 g Protein; 820 mg Sodium

Herb and Garlic Spaghetti Squash Noodles

These noodles are a nice change from your usual wheat pasta. You will probably need to batch cook the squash depending on how large it is. Most air fryer models will fit only half a squash at a time. Serve with a fresh garden salad on the side.

Large spaghetti squash	1	1
Olive oil	1 tbsp.	15 mL
Salt	1/2 tsp.	2 mL
Butter	3 tbsp.	45 mL
Large shallot, diced	1	1
Garlic cloves, sliced	3	3
Half and half cream	1/2 cup	125 ml
Chopped fresh basil	1 tbsp.	15 mL
Chopped fresh parsley	2 tbsp.	30 mL
Grated Parmesan cheese	1 cup	250 mL
Salt	1 tsp.	5 mL
Black pepper	1 tsp.	5 mL

Chopped fresh parsley, for garnish

Trim ends of squash and then cut in half lengthwise. Scoop out and discard seeds. Rub olive oil onto exposed flesh of squash and season with first amount of salt. Cook each half at 400°F (200°C) for 12 minutes. Let stand until cool enough to handle.

For the sauce, melt butter on medium heat in a medium frying pan. Add shallots and cook for 2 minutes. Add garlic and cook for 1 minute. Add cream, basil, first amount of parsley and Parmesan and bring to a boil. Reduce temperature and simmer for 10 minutes, stirring occasionally. Season with salt and pepper.

Transfer squash to a clean work surface. Drag a fork lengthwise down flesh to loosen strands. Divide strands between 4 plates and top with sauce. Garnish with remaining parsley and serve immediately. Makes 4 servings.

Combo air fryer: Cook each half for 20 minutes.

1 serving: 380 Calories; 24 g Total Fat (7 g Mono, 2 g Poly, 13 g Sat); 60 mg Cholesterol; 31 g Carbohydrate (5 g Fibre, 1 g Sugar); 14 g Protein; 1420 mg Sodium

Pulled Jackfruit Quesadillas

All the flavour of pulled pork but with shredded jackfruit in place of the meat! We thought air-fried quesadillas would be a more interesting way to eat the pulled jackfruit, instead of the bun typically seen in pulled pork sandwiches, and boy were we right!

Butter	1 tbsp.	15 mL
Olive oil	1 tbsp.	15 mL
Small white onion, thinly sliced	1	1
Medium green pepper, thinly sliced	1	1
Garlic clove, minced	1	1
Brown sugar	1 tsp.	5 mL
Can of jackfruit in brine (19 oz., 540 mL), core removed	2	2
Barbecue sauce	1/2 cup	125 mL
Water	1/2 cup	125 mL
Worcestershire sauce	1 tsp.	5 mL
Paprika	1/2 tsp.	2 mL
Salt	1/2 tsp.	2 mL
Pepper	1/2 tsp.	2 mL
Grated Monterey Jack cheese	1 cup	250 mL
Grated Edam cheese	1 cup	250 mL
Flour tortillas (9 inch, 23 cm, in diameter)	4	4

Heat butter and oil in a large frying pam on medium-low. Add onion and green pepper and cook for 15 to 18 minutes, stirring occasionally, until onions begin to caramelize.

Add garlic and brown sugar and cook until fragrant, about 2 minutes.

Stir in next 7 ingredients and bring to a boil. Reduce heat to a simmer and cook, covered, for about 20 to 25 minutes, stirring occasionally. Remove lid and mash jackfruit with a potato masher, until jackfruit takes on a pulled pork look. Cook for another 5 minutes, until jackfruit is heated through.

Combine both cheeses in a medium bowl.

Lay tortillas on a clean work surface and divide jackfruit mixture evenly among them, putting it only on one side of the tortilla. Top jackfruit with cheese mixture. Fold tortilla over, creating a half moon shape, pressing down firmly. Spray both sides with vegetable oil spray. Transfer one to air fryer. Cook at 350°F (175°C) for 12 minutes, flipping halfway through. Repeat with remaining quesadillas. Cut each quesadilla into 3 pieces. Makes 4 servings.

Combo air fryer: Cook for 12 minutes, flipping halfway through.

1 serving: 670 Calories; 33 g Total Fat (8 g Mono, 1.5 g Poly, 14 g Sat); 60 mg Cholesterol; 71 g Carbohydrate (7 g Fibre, 3 g Sugar); 24 g Protein; 1870 mg Sodium

Chilies Rellenos

We've used poblano peppers for this dish but you could also use jalapeño peppers, if you prefer.

Poblano peppers, seeds removed, stem intact (see Tip, page 28)	4	4
Olive oil	1/4 cup	60 mL
Medium white onion, thinly sliced	1	1
Garlic cloves, diced	2	2
Chipotle chili powder	1 tsp.	5 mL
Can of whole plum tomatoes (28 oz., 796 mL)	1	1
Ground cumin	1 tsp.	5 mL
Salt	1/2 tsp.	2 mL
Lime juice	1 tsp.	5 mL
Chopped fresh cilantro	1/4 cup	60 mL
Large eggs, whites and yolks separated	6	6
All-purpose flour	1 cup	250 mL
Salt	1 tsp.	5 mL
Dry bread crumbs (see Tip, page 134)	2 cups	500 mL
Grated Monterey Jack cheese with jalapeño	2 cups	500 mL
Grated Edam cheese	1 cup	250 mL
Sour cream	1/2 cup	125 mL

Cut a T shape in each pepper, starting at stem and continuing to tip. Remove seeds, being careful not to tear chili. Cook at 400°F (200°C) for 10 minutes, flipping halfway through. Transfer to a bowl, cover with plastic wrap and let stand for 7 minutes to loosen skins. Peel and discard skins. Set peppers aside.

For the sauce, in a medium frying pan, heat oil on medium-high. Add onion and cook until softened, about 5 minutes. Reduce heat to medium-low. Add next 7 ingredients and simmer for 20 minutes. Blend with an immersion blender until combined but still chunky.

Beat egg whites with an electric hand mixer on high until a stiff peak forms, about 3 to 5 minutes. Reduce speed to low and add in egg yolks, one at a time, until incorporated. Mixture should be fluffy and golden.

In a shallow dish, combine flour and salt. Measure bread crumbs into a separate dish.

Combine both cheeses and sour cream in a medium bowl. Fill each pepper with mixture and secure with a toothpick. Dip first into flour, then into egg mixture, and finally into bread crumbs. Spray with olive oil and cook at 400°F (200°C) for 12 minutes. To serve, spoon a dollop of tomato sauce on 4 plates and top each with a chili. Serve immediately. Makes 4 chilies.

Combo air fryer: Cook peppers for 10 minutes, flipping halfway through. Cook filled, breaded peppers for 12 minutes.

1 chili: 900 Calories; 51 g Total Fat (16 g Mono, 4 g Poly, 22 g Sat); 395 mg Cholesterol; 72 g Carbohydrate (6 g Fibre, 12 g Sugar); 38 g Protein; 2100 mg Sodium

Veggie Tempura

Thin batters don't work well in the air fryer, so the batter for this dish is thicker than you might expect for tempura. Feel free to switch up the vegetables to include your favouites.

All-purpose flour	1 cup	250 mL
Cornstarch	2 tbsp.	30 mL
Salt	1/2 tsp.	2 mL
Chinese five spice powder	1 tsp.	5 mL
Garlic powder	1/2 tsp.	2 mL
Water	1 cup	250 mL
Egg yolk	1	1
Egg whites, lightly beaten	2	2
Dry bread crumbs (see Tip, below)	1 cup	250 mL
Green beans	1/2 cup	125 mL
Broccoli florets, bite size	2 cups	500 mL
Medium zucchini, cut into 1 inch (2.5 cm) circles	1	1
Medium yam, cut into 1 inch (2.5 cm) circles	1/2	1/2

Combine first 5 ingredients in a large mixing bowl. Make a well in centre and add water and egg yolk. Stir until flour mixture is wet. Add egg whites and stir until just combined.

Measure bread crumbs into a separate shallow dish. Dip vegetable pieces, one at a time, into batter and then into bread crumbs. Place coated veggies into air fryer basket and spray each piece with vegetable oil spray. Cook at 400°F (200°C) for 10 minutes, flipping halfway through. Makes 4 servings.

Combo air fryer: Cook for 10 minutes, flipping halfway through.

1 serving: 320 Calories; 3 g Total Fat (0.5 g Mono, 0 g Poly, 1 g Sat); 50 mg Cholesterol; 63 g Carbohydrate (6 g Fibre, 5 g Sugar); 13 g Protein; 690 mg Sodium

Tip: To make dry bread crumbs, remove the crusts from slices of two-day old bread. Leave the bread on the counter for a day or two until it's dry, or, if you are in a hurry, set the bread slices on a baking sheet and bake on a 200°F (95°C) oven, turning occasionally until dry. Break the bread into pieces and process until crumbs reach the desired fineness. One slice of bread will make about 1/4 cup (60 mL) fine dry bread crumbs. Freeze extra bread crumbs in an airtight container or in a resealable freezer bag.

Butternut Squash Fritters

We've put these in the sides section, but really, they would be great as appetizers, snacks or even an alternative to hash browns for breakfast! As a side they would pair well with grilled or baked chicken or fish, or try them with the Lemon Herb Turkey Breasts (p. 100). They are excellent dipped in jalapeño jelly.

All-purpose flour	2 cups	500 mL
Grated Cheddar cheese	1 cup	250 mL
Baking powder	1 tbsp.	15 mL
Garlic powder	1 tsp.	10 mL
Onion powder	1 tsp.	10 mL
Paprika	1/2 tsp.	2 mL
Salt	1 tsp.	5 mL
Cooked butternut squash (see Note)	2 cups	500 mL
Large eggs, fork beaten	2	2
Sliced green onions	3 tbsp.	45 mL
Buttermilk (see Tip, page 40)	1/2 cup	125 mL

Combine first 7 ingredients in a medium bowl.

Place squash in a clean dish towel and squeeze out as much liquid as possible. Add to flour mixture along with eggs and green onion. Stir until well combined.

Slowly mix in buttermilk until batter is stiff. Batter should hold shape. Using 3 tbsp. (45 mL) for each, scoop batter into mounds on a baking sheet lined with parchment paper. Let stand in refrigerator for 1 hour. Line air fryer basket with air fryer parchment paper. Spray mounds with vegetable oil spray and transfer to basket, reshaping into mounds if necessary. Cook at 400°F (200°C) until a wooden pick inserted into centre comes out clean, about 12 to 14 minutes, flipping halfway through. Serve hot. Makes 16 fritters.

Combo air fryer: Cook for 24 minutes, flipping halfway through.

Note: To cook butternut squash in the air fryer, cut it in half and remove the seeds. Pierce the skin side of squash all over. Spray with vegetable oil spray and cook at 375°F (190°C) until soft, about 28 to 30 minutes (about 40 minutes for combo air fryer). Set aside to cool before removing flesh.

1 fritter: 100 Calories; 3 g Total Fat (1 g Mono, 0 g Poly, 1.5 g Sat); 35 mg Cholesterol; 14 g Carbohydrate (0 g Fibre, 0 g Sugar); 4 g Protein; 260 mg Sodium

Hasselback Potatoes

Hasselback potatoes are a potato lover's dream. Perfectly crispy on the edges, creamy in the middle and rich and buttery overall. Topped with bacon, sour cream, cheese and chives, these potatoes are a real game changer.

Double smoked bacon slices, chopped	4	4
Medium russet potatoes	4	4
Butter, melted	1/4 cup	60 mL
Garlic powder	1/4 tsp.	1 mL
Salt	1/4 tsp.	1 mL
Black pepper	1/4 tsp.	1 mL
Chopped fresh chives	5 tbsp.	75 mL
Grated white Cheddar cheese	2 cups	500 mL

Place bacon in air fryer basket and cook at 350°F (175°C) for 14 minutes. Transfer to a plate lined with paper towel to drain.

Place 1 potato on a large spoon. Cut crosswise into 1/4 inch (6 mm) thick slices just to edge of spoon, leaving bottom of potato uncut. Place in a bowl of cold water. Repeat with remaining potatoes. When all are cut, drain and pat potatoes dry.

Combine melted butter and garlic powder. Brush butter mixture over each potato and into every cut. Season with salt and pepper. Cook for 15 minutes. Brush again with butter making sure to get it inside fanned out slices. Cook for 25 minutes, flipping halfway through, until potatoes are browned and cooked through.

Brush with butter again and top with bacon, cheese and chives. Serve immediately. Makes 4 potatoes.

Combo air fryer: Cook bacon for 14 minutes. Cook potatoes for 15 minutes. Brush with butter and cook for 30 minutes, flipping halfway through.

1 potato: 670 Calories; 48 g Total Fat (16 g Mono, 3 g Poly, 25 g Sat); 115 mg Cholesterol; 39 g Carbohydrate (4 g Fibre, 2 g Sugar); 23 g Protein; 910 mg Sodium

Zucchini Skins

With these skins in your recipe repertoire, you will welcome the bountiful zucchini that overruns your garden every summer!

Medium zucchini	2	2
Chili powder	1/2 tsp.	2 mL
Salt	1/2 tsp.	2 mL
Ground cumin	1/4 tsp.	1 mL
Black pepper	1/4 tsp.	1 mL
Diced onion	1/2 cup	125 mL
Diced bacon slices	3	3
Chopped fresh white mushrooms	1/4 cup	60 mL
Garlic cloves, minced	2	2
Grated Cheddar cheese	1 cup	250 mL
Sour cream	1/2 cup	125 mL
Sliced green onions	2	2

Slice zucchinis in half lengthwise. Using a spoon, scrape out seeds and flesh, leaving a 1/4 inch (6 mm) border. Chop flesh and set aside. Cut each half into 3 pieces and spray with vegetable oil.

Combine next 4 ingredients and sprinkle on cut side of zucchini shells. Transfer to air fryer basket and cook at 350°F (175°C) until they begin to soften, about 4 minutes. Remove from air fryer and set aside.

Heat a medium frying pan on medium. Add onion and bacon and cook until onion softens, and bacon begins to crisp up. Transfer onion and bacon to a medium bowl and discard all but 2 tsp. (10 mL) of bacon grease. Add chopped zucchini and mushrooms, and cook for 6 to 8 minutes, stirring occasionally, until all liquids are evaporated. Stir in garlic and cook until fragrant, about 2 minutes. Return onion and bacon to pan and stir well.

Spoon bacon mixture evenly into zucchini sections. Transfer to air fryer basket and cook at 350°F (175°C) for 4 minutes. Sprinkle with cheese and cook until cheese is melted and bacon is crispy, about 2 minutes. Let stand for 3 minutes, then garnish with sour cream and green onion. Makes 12 skins.

Combo air fryer: Cook zucchini shells for 8 minutes, without disturbing. Add bacon mixture and cook for 8 minutes, then add cheese and cook for 2 minutes.

1 skin: 110 Calories; 10 g Total Fat (5 g Mono, 3.5 g Poly, 0.5 g Sat); 20 mg Cholesterol; 2 g Carbohydrate (0 g Fibre, 0 g Sugar); 4 g Protein; 250 mg Sodium

Cauliflower Arancini

Cauliflower takes the place of the traditional rice in these crispy balls stuffed with gooey mozzarella cheese. Serve with warm marinara sauce for dipping.

Large head of cauliflower, chopped	1	1
Olive oil	1 tbsp.	15 mL
Chicken broth	3 tbsp.	45 mL
Grated Parmesan cheese	1/4 cup	60 mL
Grated mozzarella cheese	1/2 cup	125 mL
Salt	1/4 tsp.	1 mL
Black pepper	1/4 tsp.	1mL
Large egg	1	1
Mozzarella cheese cubes (3/4 inch, 2 cm, each)	8	8
Large egg	1	1
Dry bread crumbs (see Tip, page 134)	1/2 cup	125 mL
Finely grated Parmesan cheese		
Dried oregano	1 tsp.	5 mL
Salt	1/4 tsp.	1 mL
Chopped fresh parsley	1 tbsp.	15 mL

In a food processor, process cauliflower until it looks like rice. Heat oil in a frying pan on medium-high heat. Add 3 cups (750 mL) cauliflower rice (reserve any extra for another use) and cook until tender, about 7 minutes. If it gets too dry, add broth 1 tbsp. (15 mL) at a time, allowing broth to evaporate before adding more (you may not use all of the broth). Remove from heat.

Add Parmesan, mozzarella, salt and pepper and stir until cheese melts and binds mixture together. Set aside to cool slightly.

Stir in first egg. Shape mixture into 8 balls. Stuff a mozzarella cube into each ball and roll to enclose.

Whisk remaining egg in a small bowl.

Combine next 4 ingredients in a shallow dish. Dip 1 ball at a time into egg until completely coated, shaking off excess egg. Coat each ball with bread crumbs. Let stand in refrigerator for at least 1 hour. Spray with vegetable oil spray and reshape balls, if necessary. Cook at 400°F (200°C) for 20 minutes, flipping halfway through. Garnish with chopped parsley. Makes 8 arancini.

Combo air fryer: Cook for 30 minutes, flipping halfway through.

1 arancini: 260 Calories; 16 g Total Fat (5 g Mono, 1 g Poly, 9 g Sat); 75 mg Cholesterol; 13 g Carbohydrate (2 g Fibre, 3 g Sugar); 17 g Protein; 590 mg Sodium

Sage and Onion Stuffing Balls

Stuffing has never been so fun! These tasty balls are great nestled on the plate next to your turkey at Thanksgiving or Christmas, but they are also fun appetizers.

Butter	3 tbsp.	45 mL
Finely chopped onion	1/2 cup	125 mL
Finely chopped celery	1/4 cup	60 mL
Garlic cloves, minced	3	3
Day old white bread, cut into 1 inch (2.5 cm) cubes	5 cups	1.25 L
Chopped fresh sage	1/2 cup	125 mL
Chicken broth	1/4 cup	60 mL
Large egg, beaten	1	1
Poultry seasoning	1/2 tsp.	2 mL
Black pepper	1/4 tsp.	1

In a medium frying pan, heat butter on medium until melted. Add onion and celery and cook for about 5 minutes, until softened but not brown. Add garlic and cook until fragrant, about 1 minute. Remove from heat and set aside to cool.

In a large bowl combine bread cubes, onion mixture and next 5 ingredients. Mix well, ensuring that all bread cubes are evenly coated with wet ingredients and seasonings are evenly distributed. Form into 6 equal balls and refrigerate for 1 hour until firm. Spray stuffing balls lightly with vegetable oil spray and transfer to air fryer tray. Cook at 360°F (180°C) 12 minutes, flipping halfway through. Transfer to a rack and cool for 4 minutes before serving. Makes 6 stuffing balls.

Combo air fryer: Cook for 14 minutes, flipping halfway through.

1 ball: 130 Calories; 6 g Total Fat (1.5 g Mono, 0 g Poly, 4 g Sat); 15 mg Cholesterol; 18 g Carbohydrate (1 g Fibre, 0 g Sugar); 3 g Protein; 220 mg Sodium

Bacon and Pomegranate Brussels Sprouts

If you thought roasting was the only way to cook Brussels sprouts, think again! This dish will convince you to forego the oven and reach for the air fryer instead.

Olive oil	2 tbsp.	30 mL
Maple syrup	1 tbsp.	15 mL
Salt	1 tsp.	5 mL
Black pepper	1/2 tsp.	2 mL
Brussel sprouts, halved	1 1/2 lbs.	680 g
Bacon slices, chopped	3	3
Pomegranate seed	3 tbsp.	45 mL
Toasted pine nuts	3 tbsp.	45 mL
Maple syrup	1 tbsp.	15 mL

Combine first 4 ingredients in a small bowl. Mix well.

Combine Brussels sprouts and bacon pieces in a medium bowl. Add olive oil mixture and toss to coat evenly. Cook at 400°F (200°C) until Brussel sprouts are crispy and bacon is cooked through, about 10 minutes, stirring or shaking basket halfway through. Transfer to a serving dish.

Add pomegranate seeds, toasted pine nuts and maple syrup, and toss until well combined. Makes 6 servings.

Combo air fryer: Cook for 15 minutes, stirring or shaking basket every 5 minutes.

1 serving: 200 Calories; 16 g Total Fat (8 g Mono, 3 g Poly, 3.5 g Sat); 15 mg Cholesterol; 12 g Carbohydrate (3 g Fibre, 5 g Sugar); 6 g Protein; 570 mg Sodium

Lemony Asparagus with Almonds and Capers

Asparagus from the air fryer is the ideal combination of tender and crispy. With the addition of lemon and capers, this asparagus makes a nice, light, tangy side that pairs well with pretty much any meat dish.

Asparagus spears, trimmed of tough ends	36	36
Olive oil	2 tbsp.	30 mL
Salt	1/4 tsp.	1 mL
Butter	1/4 cup	30 mL
Sliced almonds	1/4 cup	60 mL
Capers	1/4 cup	60 mL
Lemon juice	2 tsp.	10 mL
Grated Parmesan cheese, optional	1/4 cup	60 mL

Combine asparagus, olive oil and salt in a large bowl, tossing well to coat. Cook at 350°F (175°C) for 8 minutes, flipping halfway through.

In a small saucepan, heat butter on medium. When butter begins to bubble, add almonds, capers and lemon juice. Cook for 2 minutes, stirring often. Transfer asparagus to a serving dish and drizzle with butter sauce. Top with parmesan cheese and serve immediately. Makes 4 servings.

Combo air fryer: Cook for 10 minutes, flipping halfway through.

1 serving: 200 Calories; 18 g Total Fat (9 g Mono, 2 g Poly, 6 g Sat); 20 mg Cholesterol; 7 g Carbohydrate (4 g Fibre, 3 g Sugar); 7 g Protein; 690 mg Sodium

Double Air-fried Fries

We use the double-fry method for these fries, like professional kitchens do, without the deep fryer or pot of oil. The result is restaurant-worthy fries, golden and crisp on the outside and perfectly cooked inside. For best results, make sure your fries are all cut to the same size so they cook evenly.

Medium russet potatoes	2	2
Vegetable oil	2 tbsp.	30 mL
Salt	1 tsp.	5 mL

Cut potatoes into 1/4 inch (6 mm) thick sticks. Soak in cool water for at least 20 minutes, up to an hour. Rinse fries in a colander until water comes out clear. Dry completely.

In a clean bowl, toss fries with 1 tbsp. (15 mL) vegetable oil. Cook at 350°F (175°C) for 15 minutes, shaking basket every 5 minutes.

Remove fries to a bowl and toss with remaining vegetable oil. Return to air fryer basket and cook for 10 minutes, shaking basket halfway through. Toss with salt and serve. Makes 4 servings.

Combo air fryer: Cook for 20 minutes, shaking basket every 5 minutes. Remove from air fryer and toss with remaining vegetable oil. Cook for 12 minutes, shaking basket halfway through. Toss with salt and serve.

1 serving: 140 Calories; 7 g Total Fat (3 g Mono, 2 g Poly, 1 g Sat); 0 mg Cholesterol; 19 g Carbohydrate (2 g Fibre, 0 g Sugar); 2 g Protein; 5 mg Sodium

Uncoated Fries

	Main Ingredient	Oil
Sweet Potato Fries	sweet potatoes cut into 1/4 inch (6 mm) sticks	vegetable oil spray
Jicama Fries	jicama cut into 1/4 inch (6 mm) sticks	vegetable oil
Parsnip Fries	parsnips cut into 1/4 inch (6 mm) sticks	avocado oil
Carrot Fries	various coloured carrots cut into 1/4 inch (6 mm) sticks	vegetable oil spray
Beet Fries	beets cut into 1/4 inch (6 mm) sticks	vegetable oil spray

- Make sure the fries are spaced out in the tray and in a single layer or they won't get crispy.
- Spray the fries evenly with vegetable oil spray or toss with oil before cooking.
- Flip the fries, or shake the basket, halfway through the cooking time.

Spice Mixture	Temp.	Cooking Time (minutes)*	Special Instructions
cornstarch, paprika, garlic powder, dried crushed chilies, salt, pepper	400°F (200°C)	10/20	soak sweet potatoes for 60 minutes and dry well before seasoning
garlic powder, onion powder, salt, dried parsley, lemon pepper, paprika	400°F (200°C)	20/40	
garlic powder, turmeric, dried parsley, salt	400°F (200°C)	10/12	drizzle cooked fries with additional honey
cornstarch, cumin, salt, dried crushed chilies, honey	325°F (160°C)	26/24	sprinkle cooked fries with fresh dill and crumbled feta
dried dill, salt, cornstarch	325°F (160°C)	20/20	

* dedicated air fryer time/combo air fryer time

Breaded Fries

	Main Ingredient	Spice Mixture
Avocado Fries	avocadoes cut into 1/2 inch (12 mm) wedges	flour, garlic powder, paprika, salt, pepper
Portobello Fries	portobello mushrooms cut into 1/4 inch (6 mm) strips	flour, paprika, salt, pepper
Mozza Sticks	mozzarella cheese sticks, cut 4 inch (10 cm) long, 1/2 inch (12 mm) wide, frozen	flour, salt, pepper
Onion Rings	sweet onion cut into 1/2 inch (2.5 cm) slices, separated into rings	flour, garlic powder, onion powder, smoked paprika, salt
Zucchini Fries	zucchini cut into 4 inch (10 cm) long, 1/2 inch (12 mm) wide sticks	flour, Italian seasoning, garlic powder, salt

- Make sure the fries are spaced out in the tray and in a single layer or they won't get crispy.
- Spray the fries evenly with vegetable oil spray or toss with oil before cooking.
- Flip the fries, or shake the basket, halfway through the cooking time.

Binder	Coating	Temp.	Cooking Time (minutes)*
egg	panko bread crumbs	400°F (200°C)	7/9
1 egg per 1 tbsp. (15 mL) milk mixture	panko bread crumbs, Parmesan cheese, fresh parsley	360°F (180°C)	7/10
1 egg per 1 tbsp. (15 mL) milk mixture	panko bread crumbs	400°F (200°C)	6/10
1 egg per 1 tbsp. (15 mL) milk mixture	dry bread crumbs	375°F (190°C)	10/12
1 egg per 1 tbsp. (15 mL) milk mixture	mix of panko and dry bread crumbs, Parmesan cheese	400°F (200°C)	7/8

* dedicated air fryer time/combo air fryer time

Fried Pickle Chips

Crunchy and salty with great dill flavour, fried pickles are a carnival food favourite. Our pickles are lighter than traditional fried pickles thanks to the air fryer, which eliminates the need for much of the oil you would find in the deep-fried version. Serve these beauties with Ranch Dip (page 166) or dressing.

Dill pickle slices, cut 1/4 inch (6 mm) thick	2 cups	500 mL
Flour	1/2 cup	125 mL
Garlic powder	1 tsp.	5 mL
Salt	1 tsp.	5 mL
Dried dill	1/2 tsp.	2 mL
Black pepper	1/2 tsp.	2 mL
Large egg	1	1
Buttermilk (see Tip, page 40)	1/4 cup	60 mL
Panko bread crumbs	2 cups	500 mL

Dry pickle slices completely.

Combine next 5 ingredients in a shallow bowl.

Beat egg and buttermilk together in a bowl.

Place panko bread crumbs in separate shallow bowl. Coat pickle slices in flour mixture, shaking off any excess. Dip into egg mixture and place in bread crumbs, turning until evenly coated. Spray breaded pickles evenly with vegetable oil spray. Cook at 400°F (200°C) until pickles are crispy and brown, about 10 minutes, flipping halfway through. Remove and set aside for 5 minutes to cool. Makes 6 servings.

Combo air fryer: Cook for 12 minutes, flipping halfway through.

1 serving: 120 Calories; 2 g Total Fat (0.5 g Mono, 0 g Poly, 0 g Sat); 35 mg Cholesterol; 21 g Carbohydrate (1 g Fibre, 2 g Sugar); 4 g Protein; 940 mg Sodium

Tomatillo Salsa with Tortilla Chips

This tangy salsa comes together quickly in the air fryer and pairs perfectly with our homemade tortilla chips. If you prefer your salsa with more heat, leave the jalapeño whole, removing the stem and keeping the seeds.

Tomatillos, husks removed	9	9
Jalapeño pepper, seed and ribs removed (see Tip, page 28)	1/2	1/2
Garlic cloves, whole	5	5
Chopped onion	3/4 cup	175 mL
Lime juice	1/3 cup	75 mL
White vinegar	3 tbsp.	45 mL
Granulated sugar	2 tbsp.	30 mL
Dried oregano	1 tsp.	15 mL
Ground cumin	1 tsp.	15 mL
Salt	1/4 tsp.	60 mL
Black pepper	1/4 tsp.	60 mL
Chopped fresh cilantro	3 tbsp.	45 mL
Small corn or flour tortillas, (6 inches, 15 cm, diameter)	5	5
Salt	1 tsp.	5 mL

Rinse tomatillos well and remove core. Spray tomatillos and jalapeño with vegetable oil spray. Cook at 200°F (400°C) for 8 minutes, flipping halfway through. Add garlic cloves and cook for another 2 minutes. Set aside to cool for 5 minutes.

Combine next 8 ingredients in a food processor. Add tomatillos, jalapeño and garlic cloves and process until smooth. Transfer to a bowl and stir in cilantro. Serve at room temperature or let stand in refrigerator for 1 hour to allow flavours to blend then bring to room temperature before serving. Makes about 3 cups (750 mL).

For the chips, spray tortillas with vegetables oil spray on each side and season with salt. Cut into 6 triangles. Transfer to air fryer basket in a single layer. Cook at 350°F (175°C) until golden brown and crispy, about 5 minutes, flipping halfway through. Set aside to cool. Serve with salsa. Makes 30 chips.

Combo air fryer: Cook tomatillos and jalapeño for 12 minutes, flipping halfway through. Add garlic cloves and cook for another 2 minutes. Cook chips for 7 minutes, flipping halfway through.

1/2 cup (125 mL) salsa and 5 tortilla chips: 130 Calories; 4 g Total Fat (1.5 g Mono, 1.5 g Poly, 0.5 g Sat); 0 mg Cholesterol; 23 g Carbohydrate (3 g Fibre, 8 g Sugar); 2 g Protein; 500 mg Sodium

Baba Ganoush with Pita Chips

Homemade pita chips are quick and simple thanks to the air fryer. They pair perfectly with this creamy, garlicky baba ganoush. Together they are the perfect snack and a great addition to any mezze platter.

Medium eggplant (about 1 lb., 454 g)	1	1
Olive oil	2 tsp.	10 mL
Tahini	3 tbsp.	45 mL
Lemon juice	2 tbsp.	30 mL
Garlic cloves, minced	3	3
Salt	1/2 tsp.	2 mL
Ground cumin	1/4 tsp.	1 mL
Smoked paprika	1/8 tsp.	0.5 mL
Extra virgin olive oil, optional	1 tbsp.	15 mL
Pomegranate seeds	1 tbsp.	15 mL
Chopped fresh parsley	2 tsp.	10 mL
Pita pockets	4	4
Olive oil	1 tbsp.	15 mL
Salt	1/2 tsp.	2 mL
Black pepper	1/2 tsp.	2 mL

Cut eggplant in half lengthwise, removing stem. Prick holes in skin with a fork. Brush flesh sides with olive oil and transfer to air fryer tray. Cook at 400°F (200°C) until flesh is browned, about 20 minutes.

Transfer eggplant to a plate and set aside until cool enough to handle. Scoop flesh of both halves into a food processor, discarding skin. Add next 6 ingredients and pulse food processor on and off for about 20 seconds. Mixture should be well pureed but not completely smooth.

Transfer to a bowl and drizzle with second amount of olive oil, if using. Garnish with pomegranate seeds and parsley. Makes about 2 cups (500 mL).

For the chips, cut pita pockets into 8 triangles. Place in a large resealable plastic bag. Drizzle with olive oil and salt and pepper. Shake bag to ensure everything is coated. Transfer to air fryer tray in a single layer. Cook at 325°F (160°C) for 6 minutes, flipping halfway through. Set aside to cool for about 10 minutes. Serve with baba ganoush. Makes 32 pita chips.

Combo air fryer: Cook eggplant for 20 minutes, flipping halfway through. Cook chips for 6 minutes, flipping halfway through.

1/2 cup (125 mL) baba ganoush and 8 pita chips: 320 Calories; 16 g Total Fat (7 g Mono, 1 g Poly, 2 g Sat); 0 mg Cholesterol; 38 g Carbohydrate (6 g Fibre, 5 g Sugar); 9 g Protein; 720 mg Sodium

Chipotle Aioli

Rich and thick with a touch of heat from the chipotle chili pepper, this sauce will add panache to any burger, or serve it as a dip for the fries or chips in this book. It pairs especially well with sweet potato fries.

Mayonnaise	1/2 cup	125 mL
Finely chopped chives	2 tbsp.	30 mL
Garlic cloves, minced	2	2
Lime juice	2 tsp.	10 mL
Chipotle chili powder	1 tsp.	5 mL
Salt, to taste		
Black pepper, to taste		

Whisk first 5 ingredients together. Season with salt and pepper, if needed. Let stand in refrigerator until ready to serve. Makes about 1/2 cup (125 mL).

2 tbsp. (30 mL): 100 Calories; 10 g Total Fat (6 g Mono, 3 g Poly, 1 g Sat); 0 mg Cholesterol; 0 g Carbohydrate (0 g Fibre, 0 g Sugar); 0 g Protein; 100 mg Sodium

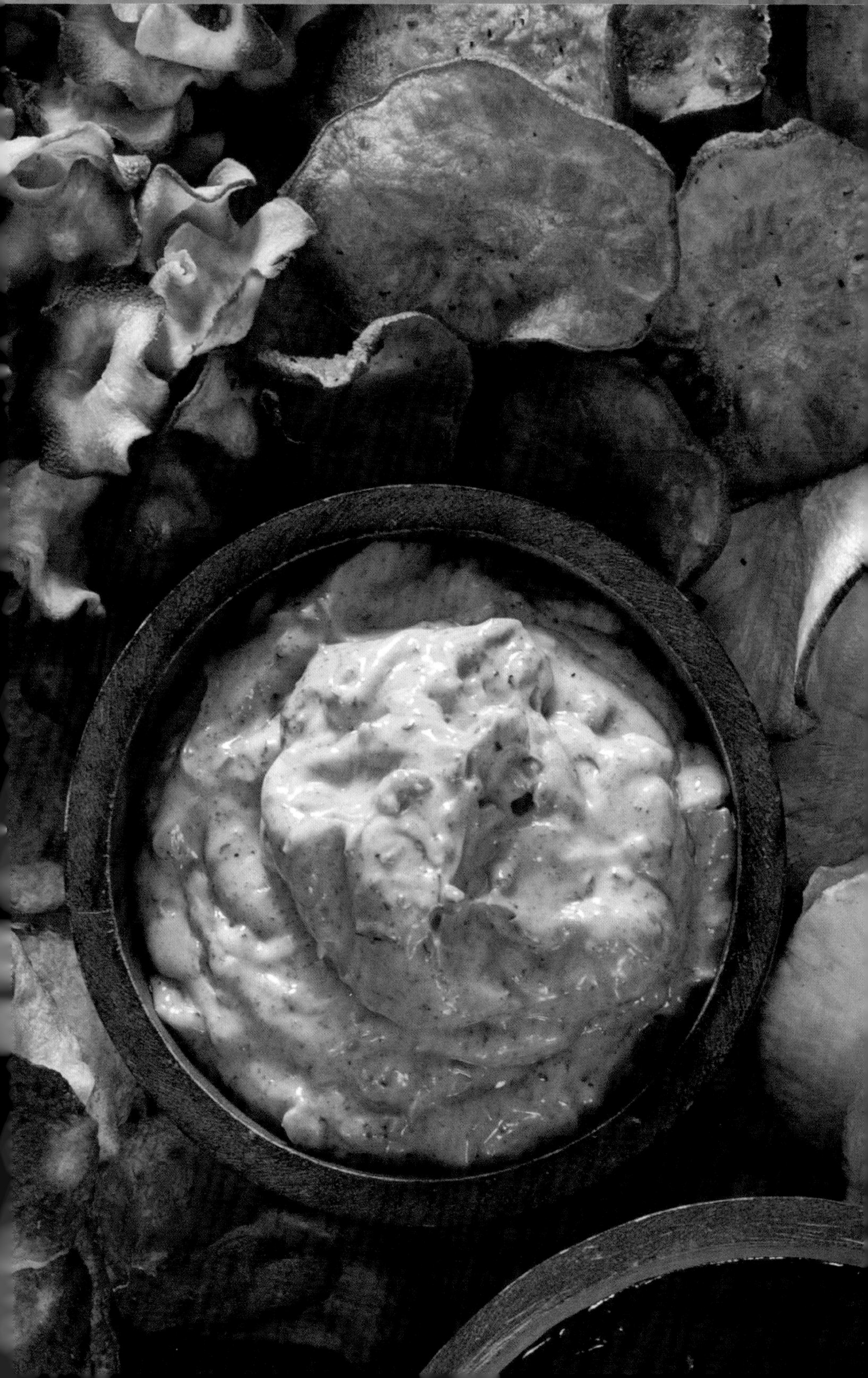

Spicy Rum Marmalade Dip

A little bit sweet and a little bit spicy, this dip is a wonderful accompaniment to many of the chips and fries in this book. It also pairs perfectly with the Coconut Prawns on page 106.

Orange marmalade	1 cup	250 mL
Orange juice	1/4 cup	60 mL
Rum	3 tbsp.	45 mL
Lime juice	1 tbsp.	15 mL
Grated ginger root	2 tsp.	10 mL
Dry mustard	1 tsp.	5 mL
Dried crushed chilies	1 tsp.	5 mL

Combine all 7 ingredients in a small saucepan on medium heat. Bring to a boil, and then reduce to a simmer. Cook for 5 minutes, stirring constantly, until slightly reduced. Remove from heat and set aside to cool. Transfer to a bowl and serve at room temperature or let stand in refrigerator for 1 hour to allow flavours to blend. Makes 1 1/2 cups (375 mL).

1/4 cup (60 mL): 160 Calories; 0 g Total Fat (0 g Mono, 0 g Poly, 0 g Sat); 0 mg Cholesterol; 37 g Carbohydrate (0 g Fibre, 33 g Sugar); 0 g Protein; 30 mg Sodium

Ranch Dip

No need to run out and buy a tub of this dip when you can make it yourself at home. It pairs especially well with the Fried Pickle Chips (page 156).

Mayonnaise	1 cup	250 mL
Buttermilk	1/4 cup	60 mL
Chopped fresh parsley	3 tbsp.	45 mL
Chopped fresh chives	2 tbsp.	30 mL
Chopped fresh dill	1 tbsp.	15 mL
Garlic cloves, minced	2	2
Onion powder	2 tsp.	10 mL
White vinegar	1/2 tsp.	2 mL
Salt	1/2 tsp.	2 mL
Pepper	1/4 tsp.	1 mL
Cayenne powder	1/8 tsp.	0.5 mL

Combine all 11 ingredients in a medium bowl. Stir well to combine. Let stand in refrigerator for at least 30 minutes to allow flavours to blend. Makes about 2 cups (500 mL).

2 tbsp. (30 mL): 130 Calories; 13 g Total Fat (8 g Mono, 4 g Poly, 1.5 g Sat); 5 mg Cholesterol; 0 g Carbohydrate (0 g Fibre, 0 g Sugar); 0 g Protein; 220 mg Sodium

Chips

	Main Ingredient	Oil
Apple Chips	Honeycrisp, Granny Smith or Gala apples cut into 1/8 inch (3 mm) slices	grapeseed oil
Pear Chips	pears cut into 1/8 inch (3 mm) slices	grapeseed oil
Kale Chips	kale trimmed into 2 inch (5 cm) inches	sesame oil
Plantain Chips	plantain cut into 1/8 inch (3 mm) slices	vegetable oil
Cassava Chips	cassava cut into 1/8 inch (3 mm) slices and soaked in cold water for 45 minutes	vegetable oil

- We recommend slicing your fruit and vegetables with a mandolin to ensure the slices are an even thickness.

- Make sure the chips are spaced out in the tray and in a single layer or they won't get crispy.

Seasoning	Temp.	Cooking Time (minutes)*
cinnamon	375°F (190°C)	12, flip every 3 / 16, flip every 4 and rotate basket
nutmeg	375°F (190°C)	14, flip every 2 / 18, flip every 3 and rotate basket
nutritional yeast, lemon zest, soy sauce, onion powder, salt	370°F (185°C)	8, toss every 2 / 16, toss every 3
salt, paprika, cumin, turmeric, pepper	350°F (175°C)	6, flip halfway / 7, flip halfway
salt	375°F (190°C)	10, stir every 2 / 14, stir every 2 and rotate basket

* dedicated air fryer time/combo air fryer time

Chips (con't)

	Main Ingredient	Oil
Taro Chips	taro cut into 1/8 inch (3 mm) slices	vegetable oil
Parsnip Chips	parsnips cut into 1/8 inch (3 mm) slices	avocado oil
Beet Fries	beets cut into 1/8 inch (3 mm) slices	vegetable oil
Potato Chips	russet potatoes cut into 1/8 inch (3 mm) slices	vegetable oil
Sweet Potato/ Yam Fries	sweet potatoes or yams cut into 1/8 inch (3 mm) slices and soaked in cold water for 20 minutes	vegetable oil

- We recommend slicing your fruit and vegetables with a mandolin to ensure the slices are an even thickness.

- Make sure the chips are spaced out in the tray and in a single layer or they won't get crispy.

Seasoning	Temp.	Cooking Time (minutes)*
salt	350°F (175°C)	10, stir every 2 / 12, stir every 3 and rotate basket
garlic powder, turmeric, salt	350°F (175°C)	6, flip every 2 / 8, flip every 2 and rotate basket
dried dill, salt	330°F (165°C)	20, flip every 5 / 25, flip every 5 and rotate basket
salt, pepper	370°F (185°C)	25, flip every 5 / 35, flip every 5 and rotate basket
dried thyme, salt, pepper, paprika	360°F (180°C)	16, flip every 4 / 18, flip every 6 and rotate basket

* dedicated air fryer time/combo air fryer time

Salted Caramel Lava Cakes

You might not think of cooking a cake in your air fryer, but you should! The end result with this recipe is a moist chocolate cake with a rich, creamy caramel centre. Yum! Garnish with fresh berries and a sprinkle of icing sugar for an attractive presentation.

Unsalted butter, cut into pieces	1/2 cup	125 mL
Semi-sweet chocolate, chopped	8 oz.	225 g
Large eggs	3	3
Granulated sugar	1/4 cup	60 mL
Vanilla extract	1 tsp.	5 mL
All-purpose flour	1/4 cup	60 mL
Cocoa, sifted if lumpy	1 tbsp.	15 mL
Caramel squares	8	8
Half and half cream	2 tbsp.	30 mL
Sea salt flakes	1 tsp.	5 mL

In a double boiler, melt butter and chocolate, stirring constantly (see Note). Set aside.

Beat eggs, sugar, and vanilla in a medium bowl. Slowly add chocolate mixture, mixing constantly until it is all incorporated. Add flour and mix until just incorporated.

Grease four 1 cup (250 mL) ramekins with vegetable oil spray and sprinkle evenly with cocoa. Divide batter between ramekins.

To soften caramels, place in a small microwave-safe bowl with cream and microwave for 30 seconds, stirring every 10 seconds. Stir in salt. Divide evenly among ramekins, spooning into centre of chocolate batter. Place ramekins into air fryer basket. Cook at 375°F (190°C) for 12 minutes, covering tops with foil halfway through. Carefully remove from air fryer and set aside to cool for about 3 minutes. Using a butter knife, loosen cakes from ramekins. To serve, place a dessert plate on top of each ramekin and invert. Remove ramekins and serve immediately. Makes 4 cakes.

Combo air fryer: Cook on lowest rack for 14 minutes, covering with foil halfway through.

1 cake: 720 Calories; 46 g Total Fat (8 g Mono, 1.5 g Poly, 28 g Sat); 225 mg Cholesterol; 73 g Carbohydrate (3 g Fibre, 59 g Sugar); 10 g Protein; 650 mg Sodium

Note: If you don't have a double boiler, melt butter and chocolate in a bowl placed over a pot of simmering (not boiling!) water.

Peach Blueberry Hand Pies

A delicious combination of peaches and blueberries tucked into a hand-held pie that has been baked to perfection in your trusty air fryer. No need for a scoop of ice cream with these pies (but of course we won't judge if you choose to add one).

All-purpose flour	2 cups	500 mL
Salt	1/2 tsp.	2 mL
Butter, cut into cubes	3/4 cup	175 mL
Cold water	6 tbsps.	90 mL
Chopped peaches, fresh or frozen	1 1/2 cups	375 mL
Blueberries, fresh or frozen	3/4 cup	175 mL
Sugar	1/2 cup	125 mL
Cornstarch	2 tsp.	10 mL
Lemon zest	1 tsp.	5 mL
Nutmeg	1/4 tsp.	1 mL
Large egg yolk, fork beaten	1	1

For the pie dough, process first 3 ingredients in food processor until mixture is crumbly (see Note). Add water and pulse with on/off motion until mixture starts to come together. Do not over process. Turn pastry out onto a work surface and knead so that a dough is formed. Divide into 2 equal portions. Wrap with plastic wrap and chill for at least 1 hour or up to overnight. Roll out first portion on a lightly floured surface to 1/8-inch (3 mm) thickness. Cut out four 5-inch (12.5 cm) circles. Set on a baking sheet lined with parchment paper and repeat with remaining pie dough. Cover with plastic wrap and chill for about 15 minutes.

For the filling, combine next 6 ingredients in a medium bowl.

Remove dough from fridge. Divide filling among dough circles. Brush egg yolk around edge of circles. Fold dough over in a half moon shape and pinch together. Crimp edge with a fork and cut slits in top. Spray with vegetable oil spray. Cook at 360°F (180°C) for 14 minutes, rotating pies halfway through. Let stand for 10 minutes before serving. Makes 8 pies.

Combo air fryer: Cook for 15 minutes, rotating basket halfway through.

Note: If you don't have a food processor, combine flour and salt in a medium bowl. Cut in butter until crumbly. Stir in water with a fork.

1 pie: 350 Calories; 19 g Total Fat (5 g Mono, 1 g Poly, 11 g Sat); 70 mg Cholesterol; 42 g Carbohydrate (2 g Fibre, 17 g Sugar); 4 g Protein; 270 mg Sodium

Honey Thyme Cheesecake

A sweet, creamy cheesy filling accented with honey and thyme is nestled into a sweet arrowroot crust. Feel free to drizzle a little more honey over top before serving.

Crushed arrowroot biscuits	1 1/2 cups	375 mL
Unsalted butter, melted	1/2 cup	125 mL
Fresh thyme leaves	1 tbsp.	15 mL
Honey	1 tbsp.	15 mL
Cream cheese	2 cups	500 mL
Lemon zest	1 tsp.	5 mL
Icing (confectioner's) sugar	1/2 cup	125 mL
Granulated sugar	1 1/2 cups	375 mL
Sour cream	2 tbsp.	30 mL
Vanilla Greek yogurt	3 tbsp.	45 mL
Honey	2 tbsp.	30 mL
Large eggs	2	2
Vanilla extract	1 tbsp.	15 mL
Fresh thyme leaves	1/2 tbsp.	7 mL

Combine biscuits, butter and first amount of thyme and honey in a large bowl. Spoon mixture into an 8 inch (20 cm) springform cake pan lined with parchment paper pan and press down to form an even layer. Cover with plastic wrap and set aside in refrigerator.

In a large bowl, combine next 9 ingredients. Pour slowly into pan and smooth over crust. Cook at 325°F (160°C) for 55 minutes. Unplug air fryer and let cake stand in air fryer for 30 minutes.

Garnish with remaining thyme. Cool in refrigerator for at least 6 hours before serving. Cuts into 8 wedges.

Combo air fryer: Cook for 60 minutes on lowest rack. Unplug air fryer and let stand for 30 minutes.

1 wedge: 640 Calories; 37 g Total Fat (3.5 g Mono, .5 g Poly, 22 g Sat); 145 mg Cholesterol; 72 g Carbohydrate (0 g Fibre, 60 g Sugar); 8 g Protein; 370 mg Sodium

Chocolate Chip Cookie Pizza

This cookie is delicious as-is, but for an extra decadent treat, you can smother it with dulce de leche (page 184) and bake for a few extra minutes, until it is crispy and gooey.

All-purpose flour	1 1/8 cups	280 mL
Baking soda	1/2 tsp.	2 mL
Salt	1/2 tsp.	2 mL
Butter, softened	6 tbsp.	90 mL
Honey	1 tbsp.	15 mL
Vanilla extract	1 tsp.	5 mL
Brown sugar	1/4 cup	60 mL
Granulated sugar	1/3 cup	75 mL
Large egg	1	1
White chocolate chips	1/2 cup	125 mL
Semi-sweet chocolate chips	1/2 cup	125 ml

In a medium bowl, whisk together flour, baking soda and salt. Set aside.

In a large bowl, beat butter with a mixer. Add honey, vanilla, brown sugar, sugar and egg and mix until creamy.

Fold in white chocolate and chocolate chips. Lightly spray a shallow 8 inch (20 cm) cake pan with vegetable oil spray. Press cookie dough evenly into dish. Cook at 360°F (180°C) for 18 minutes (see Note), rotating halfway through. Cuts into 4 wedges.

Combo air fryer: Cook for 22 minutes, rotating halfway through.

Note: Do not overbake. The cookie is best when it is slightly underbaked, as it will continue to cook a little inside even after it is removed from the air fryer.

1 wedge: 700 Calories; 35 g Total Fat (4.5 g Mono, 1 g Poly, 23 g Sat); 100 mg Cholesterol; 95 g Carbohydrate (3 g Fibre, 60 g Sugar); 7 g Protein; 630 mg Sodium

Baklava Bites

These cute little bites are even better if you save a little of the syrup to drizzle over top before serving.

Pistachios, chopped	1 cup	250 mL
Walnuts, chopped	1 cup	250 mL
Ground cinnamon	1 tbsp.	15 mL
Water	1 1/2 cups	375 mL
Granulated sugar	1 1/2 cups	375 mL
Honey	1/2 cup	125 mL
Lemon peel	2	2
Whole cloves	2	2
Phyllo pastry sheets	10	10
Unsalted butter, melted	1 cup	250 mL

Toss nuts with cinnamon and set aside. Reserve 1/4 cup (60 mL) nut mixture for garnish.

For the syrup, combine water and sugar in a medium saucepan and bring to a boil. Cook, stirring often, until sugar is dissolved. Reduce heat to medium-low and stir in honey, lemon peel and cloves. Simmer for 15 to 20 minutes. Remove from heat and set aside to cool. Remove lemon peel and cloves and discard.

On a clean work surface, unroll phyllo pastry and cover with a damp cloth to prevent them from drying out. Lay out one phyllo sheet and brush with butter. Lay another sheet on top and brush with butter. Repeat until you have 5 layers. Cut the phyllo sheets into 12 rectangles, 4 cuts widthwise and 3 cuts lengthwise Place 1 tbsp. (15 mL) of nut mixture in centre and fold pastry up on sides, leaving a little opening at top. Spoon 1 tbsp. (15 mL) syrup in opening and twist dough to seal. Place on air fryer tray and repeat with remaining pastry, filling and syrup. Brush tops with butter and bake at 325°F (160°C) until browned, about 10 minutes. Drizzle any remaining syrup over warm bites. Garnish with reserved nut mixture. Makes 24 bites.

Combo air fryer: Cook for 12 minutes, rotating basket halfway through.

1 bite: 210 Calories; 13 g Total Fat (3.5 g Mono, 3.5 g Poly, 5 g Sat); 20 mg Cholesterol; 21 g Carbohydrate (1 g Fibre, 13 g Sugar); 3 g Protein; 115 mg Sodium

Air-fried Chocolate Bars

A carnival favourite brought to your air fryer! You can use pretty much any type of chocolate bar you'd like. We went with Snickers and Mars bars because we wanted the gooey caramel. Make sure the dough covers the chocolate bar completely or the bar will melt in the air fryer and leak out of the cracks in the dough.

Packages of refrigerated crescent dough (8 count)	2	2
Miniature Snickers bars	8	8
Miniature Mars bars	8	8
Icing (confectioner's) sugar, optional	2 tbsp.	30 mL

Separate dough sections on a clean work surface and wrap each bar individually, folding corners over and making sure dough covers chocolate bar completely. Spray each with vegetable oil spray, making sure to coat all sides. Cook at 360°F (180°C) for 5 minutes. Flip each piece and cook for 3 to 5 minutes more until golden brown.

Transfer to a platter and sift powdered sugar over top if using. Makes 16 bars.

Combo air fryer: Cook for 10 minutes, flipping halfway through.

1 bar: 150 Calories; 8 g Total Fat (1 g Mono, 0 g Poly, 3 g Sat); 0 mg Cholesterol; 15 g Carbohydrate (0 g Fibre, 6 g Sugar); 3 g Protein; 230 mg Sodium

Churros

In our humble opinion, churros from the air fryer are even more delicious than their deep-fried counterparts. Serve with a chocolate sauce or dulce de leche (see sidebar, page 185) for dipping

Water	1 cup	250 mL
Unsalted butter, cut into chunks	1/2 cup	125 mL
Salt	1/2 tsp.	2 mL
All-purpose flour	1 cup	250 mL
Vanilla	1 tsp.	5 mL
Large eggs	3	3
Granulated sugar	1 cup	250 mL
Granulated sugar	1 cup	250 mL
Ground cinnamon	1 tbsp.	15 mL

In a large saucepan, combine water, first amount of butter and salt. Bring to a boil and cook, stirring occasionally, until butter is melted.

Remove mixture from heat and stir in flour, using a fork, until a thick paste forms. Stir in vanilla.

Stir in eggs, one at a time, until fully incorporated, working quickly so heat of mixture does not cook eggs.

With a spatula, stir in sugar. Transfer batter to a piping bag with a star tip or a releasable freezer bag with a corner snipped off. Pipe dough in 4 inch (10 cm) lines onto air fryer tray and spray evenly with vegetable oil spray. Cook at 400°F (200°C) for 12 minutes, flipping halfway through.

In a small bowl, combine remaining sugar and sprinkle over churros. Makes 18 churros.

Combo air fryer: Cook for 20 minutes, flipping halfway through.

1 churro with 2 tsp. (10 mL) dulce de leche: 180 Calories; 7 g Total Fat (2 g Mono, 0 g Poly, 4.5 g Sat); 55 mg Cholesterol; 27 g Carbohydrate (0 g Fibre, 26 g Sugar); 3 g Protein; 160 mg Sodium

To make your own dulce de leche, remove the label from a can of sweetened condensed milk and place the can on its side in a pot, adding enough water to cover the can entirely. Bring to boil and cook for 3 hours, adding more water as necessary to make sure the can is fully submerged. Set the can aside until cool. Transfer mixture to a bowl and stir until smooth. **Use this method only with a can that does not have a pull tab lid.** If your can has a pull tab lid, pour the contents into the top half of a double boiler (or a bowl set over a pot of boiling water) and cook until the mixture reaches the desired consistency, 2 to 3 hours, stirring often.

Baked Apples

These apples are great served with a scoop of ice cream, kind of like apple pie a la mode!

Medium tart apples, such as McIntosh	4	4
Lemon juice	1 tbsp.	15 mL
Chopped pecans	1/2 cup	125 mL
Dried cranberries	1/3 cup	75 mL
Brown sugar	1/4 cup	60 mL
Melted butter	3 tbsp.	45 mL
Ground cinnamon	1 tsp.	5 mL
Salt	1/4 tsp.	1 mL

Remove and discard stem of apple and cut about 1/2 inch (12 mm) off top. Core apple with a melon baller, leaving at least 1/2 inch (12 mm) of apple flesh around and about 1 inch (2.5 cm) from bottom, creating a well inside apple. Brush insides of apple with lemon juice.

Combine next 6 ingredients in a small bowl. Spoon into apples and cover apples with top. Transfer apples to air fryer basket and cook at 350°F (175°C) for about 8 minutes, until apples are soft. Transfer to a rack to cool for 5 minutes. Serve warm. Makes 4 apples.

Combo air fryer: Cook until apples are soft, about 15 minutes.

1 apple: 330 Calories; 16 g Total Fat (7 g Mono, 3.5 g Poly, 4.5 g Sat); 15 mg Cholesterol; 49 g Carbohydrate (7 g Fibre, 40 g Sugar); 2 g Protein; 200 mg Sodium

Strawberry Rhubarb Crisp

The classic pairing of strawberries and rhubarb with a sweet, crunchy topping flavoured with cinnamon and brown sugar. Top with a scoop of vanilla ice cream or a dollop of whipped cream for an extra treat.

Quartered strawberries	2 cups	500 mL
Sliced rhubarb	1 1/2 cups	375 mL
Sugar	1/2 cup	125 mL
Minute tapioca	1 tbsp.	15 mL
Melted butter	3 tbsp.	45 mL
Rolled oats	3/4 cup	175 mL
All-purpose flour	1/3 cup	75 mL
Brown sugar	1/2 cup	125 mL
Ground cinnamon	1 tsp.	5 mL

In a medium bowl combine first 4 ingredients. Place in a greased 1 quart (1 L) or 8 inch (20 cm) round baking dish. Cook at 400°F (200°C) until bubbling, about 7 minutes. Let mixture stand for 5 minutes.

In another medium bowl, mix next 5 ingredients until well combined. Sprinkle topping evenly over fruit and cook for 6 minutes. Carefully remove baking dish from air fryer and transfer to a wire rack. Cool for 10 minutes before serving. Makes 4 servings.

Combo air fryer: Cook until bubbling, about 10 minutes. Sprinkle with topping and cook for 10 minutes.

1 serving: 390 Calories; 7 g Total Fat (2 g Mono, 1 g Poly, 4 g Sat); 15 mg Cholesterol; 82 g Carbohydrate (5 g Fibre, 56 g Sugar); 4 g Protein; 50 mg Sodium

Index